ALBA:
THE GAELIC KINGDOM
OF SCOTLAND

Alba:

The Gaelic Kingdom of Scotland AD 800–1124

Stephen T. Driscoll

Series editor: Gordon Barclay

BIRLINN
with
HISTORIC  SCOTLAND

To Frances and Margaret

THE MAKING OF SCOTLAND *Series editor*: Gordon Barclay
Other titles available:

WILD HARVESTERS:
The First People in Scotland

FARMERS, TEMPLES AND TOMBS:
Scotland in the Neolithic and Early Bronze Age

BURGESS, MERCHANT AND PRIEST:
Burgh Life in the Scottish Medieval Town

THE AGE OF THE CLANS:
The Highlands from Somerled to the Clearances

SETTLEMENT AND SACRIFICE:
The Later Prehistoric People of Scotland

A GATHERING OF EAGLES:
Scenes from Roman Scotland

THE SEA ROAD:
A Viking Voyage through Scotland

SAINTS AND SEA-KINGS:
The First Kingdom of the Scots

ANGELS, FOOLS AND TYRANTS:
Britons and Anglo-Saxons in Southern Scotland AD 450–750

PUIR LABOURERS AND BUSY HUSBANDMEN:
The Countryside of Lowland Scotland in the Middle Ages

British Library Cataloguing-in-Publication data
A catalogue record for this book is available on request from the British Library
ISBN 1 84158 145 3
First published by Birlinn Ltd
West Newington House, 10 Newington Road, Edinburgh EH9 1QS
British Library Cataloguing-in-Publication Data
A catalogue record for this book is available on request
from the British Library
Typesetting and design by Carnegie Publishing Ltd, Lancaster
Printed and bound in Spain by Book Print SL

Contents

Sueno's Stone, Forres
Below this tower cross is a
badly weathered scene,
which some believe
represents a royal
inauguration scene.
HISTORIC SCOTLAND/
CROWN COPYRIGHT

Political Landscape and Historical Development

Dupplin Cross
View of the cross overlooking the heart of
Strathearn. The white buildings in the
middle distance are the village of Forteviot.
STEPHEN T. DRISCOLL

The events surrounding the development of the Gaelic kingdom of
Scotland, Alba, were amongst the most significant in Scottish history
and are amongst the most confusing. The period from 800 to 1100
marks a critical stage in political development of the Scottish nation
because Alba was the first kingdom to rule effectively the diverse
ethnic groups of early medieval Britain. Many of the key social and
political institutions of medieval Scotland were established at this time,
but the creative forces at work were violent and destructive. As a
consequence, historical sources from the period are in such short
supply that archaeological study of the material remains and of
significant places contributes greatly to our understanding of this era.

At the beginning of the ninth century, northern Britain was a
patchwork of small kingdoms; by the twelfth century, 'Alba', the
Gaelic kingdom of the Scots, was established as the pre-eminent
kingdom in the north. The dominion of this kingdom was centred in
the East Midlands and did not yet include the northern and Highland
districts of modern Scotland. The conquest of these outlying areas was

gradually achieved by the kings of Scots during the later Middle Ages. In cultural terms the social and institutional foundations of Alba are Celtic, but not in any pure sense. The various influences of Picts, Gaels, Britons, Angles and the Norse can all be detected. The indigenous Celtic character of this society can be clearly seen in the regional presence of the leading saints, in the distinctive artistic traditions preserved so well in sculpture, and less apparently in the organisation of the landscape, where field archaeology makes its greatest contribution.

Historical framework

Such was the level of social disruption and political upheaval during the period considered by this book that many of the key events are poorly understood and key individuals remain obscure. The use of writing and the keeping of records were severely restricted and in practice largely confined to the Church. Churchmen, particularly those in the more influential monasteries, were interested in the secular world and kept records of important events on a year by year basis. Known as annals, these records are particularly valuable because they are contemporary. The annalistic entries tend to be very brief and have a limited focus which included the deaths of great men, momentous battles, or calamities such as storms or Viking raids. Other factors also contribute to the darkness of the age (as compared with the 700s). Principal among these was the destruction of important monastic libraries and *scriptoria*, writing schools, during Viking raids. As a result, historical writing dried up and records were lost. Consequently, archaeology is crucial to our understanding of the long-term social developments and used with care is even capable of revealing ancient ideologies.

The Viking raids, which began in the 790s, were the catalyst for several centuries of endemic warfare which swept through the British Isles and remade the political map. The most notorious aspect of political violence which characterised this period, the plundering of monasteries, was widespread and not limited to the Vikings. All the major monasteries suffered devastating raids which left members of the community slain, the treasuries ransacked and buildings burnt. In terms of Scottish history, Iona was the most significant loss. Chronicles kept at Iona are widely believed to account for the presence of Scottish entries in the Irish Annals, such as the Annals of Ulster. The annalistic entries from Iona dried up, however, as the community came under increasing pressure from Viking raiders and eventually retreated to the relative safety of Kells in Meath (founded in 807). Not only were records lost, but the main conduit whereby Scottish events was introduced into the Irish Annals, one of the best historical sources, was closed.

A consequence of the closure of Iona's *scriptorium* is that there is little contemporary evidence relating to Cinaed mac Ailpín (843–58) and the circumstances surrounding his accession to the Pictish kingship. His reign is seen as a pivotal moment in the history of Scotland, although the earliest 'historical' accounts of Gaelic conqest were not composed until about 995. The description of the Gaelic triumph over the Picts clearly contains elements of myth and propaganda, but has been influential. It is not surprising that long-term cultural changes were not chronicled accurately. In the case of the demise of Pictish language and culture, it took generations before people appreciated the consequences of Cinaed's triumph and sought to explain the Gaelic ascendancy by inventing a mythological tradition of military conquest of the Picts.

The sparse nature of the evidence makes it impossible to reconstruct historical individuals and makes it difficult to interpret political strategies. This is true of even the most famous man of the age, Macbeth, who ruled Scotland from 1040 until 1057. One reason we know so little about Macbeth is because his dynasty lost the kingship and he was regarded as a usurper by the victorious faction. This prejudice is compounded by the absence of any contemporary records from Moray, Macbeth's homeland, which might have provided balance. Not surprisingly, the fictional Shakespearean character greatly overshadows the historic personage.

Although gaps in the historical record make it impossible to write a historical narrative in the traditional sense of describing important events and analysing individual actions, the major patterns are not in doubt. During the ninth century, Britain and Ireland experienced political turmoil, which can be traced to the Viking disruptions. Over the 800s, raids became longer and more sustained, the Viking war bands became larger and more organised. The Viking wars exposed fatal weaknesses in the majority of the kingdoms in Britain and most disappeared or were substantially remade. By the middle of the century their rulers began to carve out new kingdoms – in the Scottish islands, York, Dublin, and perhaps on the Clyde – from the ruins of the kingdoms they had undermined.

The instability of the ninth century created an environment which was favourable for political opportunists. Chief among these was Cinaed mac Ailpín, who despite coming from a marginal Gaelic kindred managed to seize the chief Pictish kingship in 843 and to hold it. Cinaed's dynasty managed to retain the kingship long enough to produce another leader who secured the long-term stability of this Gaelic-Pictish kingdom, Cinaed's grandson, Constantine II (900–43).

In many respects Constantine II was the real architect of medieval Scotland. He drove out the Vikings once and for all, weathered pressure from aggressive Anglo-Saxon kings, and eventually was able to retire to the comfort of the monastery at St Andrews. The kingdom he ruled was built upon the wealth of the East Midlands, but it was much smaller than modern Scotland. In the centuries that followed, Constantine's successors successfully sought to extend their authority over their neighbours to the north of the Mounth (the eastern arm of the Cairngorms), south of the Forth and into the south-west.

This military expansion saw the Gaelic cultural province expand to its widest extent in Scotland at the expense of the British kingdoms of Cumbria and Galloway, the Anglian kingdom of Northumbria and, most bitterly, Moray, which was also a Gaelic-Pictish kingdom. At the same time, Scotland weathered the pressure from the south (first Anglo-Saxon and then Norman kings) and from the Western and Northern Isles which remained a platform for Norse expansionist ambitions. By the middle of the 1000s, Scotland was the dominant power in the north and its Gaelic dynasty at the peak of its prestige, as demonstrated by the marriage of Malcolm III Canmore (1058–93) to Margaret, an Anglo-Saxon princess. Margaret is an important figure, who is credited with initiating sweeping religious reforms and introducing more European courtly practices, a process that was continued by her sons, Alexander I and David I.

Saints' cults and political identities

With the exception of Andrew, the great Scottish saints are all firmly linked to particular regions of northern Britain. For instance, the political success of the Gaelic-speaking peoples can be charted by tracing the movement of the relics of Columba from Iona to Dunkeld in 848/9 and is confirmed by the relative obscurity of the local Pictish saints, such as Serf, Ethernan and Drostan, about whom very little is known. In the south-east Cuthbert's cult spread from Melrose across the Tweed to Durham and Lindisfarne. Cuthbert's cult area corresponds to a cultural zone where native British and

Map of the Ethnic Groups
The peoples of northern Britain c. AD 800 divided into language groups with their principal religious cult centres in North Britain.
LORRAINE MACEWAN

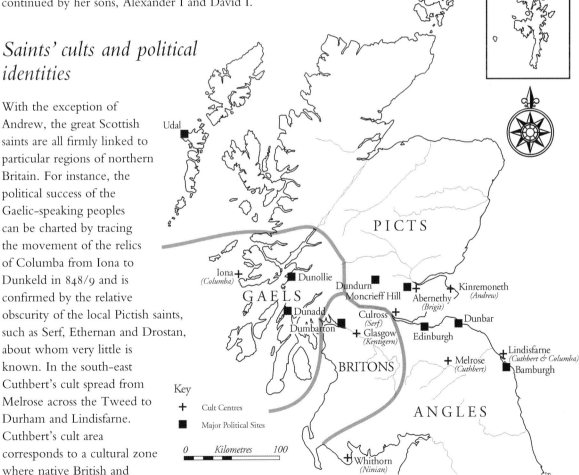

Key
+ Cult Centres
■ Major Political Sites

0 Kilometres 100

Dumbarton Rock
The twin peaks of the fort of the Britons looming over the lower Clyde.

incoming Anglian settlers mixed in the sixth century. For much of the early Middle Ages this area was politically united under Northumbrian kings. In Galloway, the Northumbrian religious élite promoted St Ninian and his ancient church at Whithorn, which remained the principal religious centre of the south-west through a sequence of rulers: British, Anglian, Norse, Gallwegian and Scottish. In the Northern Isles, not long after converting to Christianity, the Norse produced their own saint, Magnus, who was martyred in 1116.

These saints are manifestations of ethnic difference which were also apparent in languages and cultural practices. The raw material from which medieval Scotland was fashioned included a wide range of ethnic identities, geographically distinct regions and political divisions. Judging from the number of languages spoken at the time, the area of modern Scotland was the most culturally diverse region of the British Isles.

That Scotland hung together at all is even more marvellous given that the Viking Age (roughly 800–1000) saw the disappearance of most of the regional kingdoms in the British Isles. Following the initial destruction of the ninth century, a few powerful kingdoms emerged, which during the course of the next two centuries were able to consolidate their holdings and expand their territory at the expense of their neighbours. Around 900 a new kingdom, Alba, emerged in the heart of Pictland which was ruled by a Gaelic-speaking élite and formed the core of Scotland. The territorial expansion of Alba was not achieved by military might alone. Although success on the battlefield was essential, it was the institutions necessary for government which developed at this time that were to prove significant in the long run. The vigorous growth of saints' cults is perhaps the best documented of the innovative social and political developments which provided the framework for the Scottish kingdom. Alongside hereditary kinship, regional Church organisation is regarded as an essential characteristic of the medieval European state.

The means by which the king gained secure superiority over ancient regional lordships are not always clear, but, increasingly, the king relied upon legal mechanisms to rule the kingdom. At both regional and national levels, systems of estate management involving the creation of administrative districts (shires) and officials (thanes) were constructed to exploit the agricultural wealth of the East Midlands and to muster armies. The parish, the basic unit of Church administration, was intimately related to these secular systems of lordship. This is a sign that the Church was also becoming more institutionalised and political. Ancient churches began to assert superiority over surrounding parishes and eventually some of these evolved into the seats of bishops.

At the beginning of the Viking Age, northern Britain contained at least eight independent regional kingdoms whose origins may be traced back to the sixth century. These kingdoms were in a state of competitive tension: each enjoyed brief periods of superiority over their neighbours, but none achieved a permanent dominance. There was a clear ethnic basis to these kingdoms: they consisted of regions where a particular language prevailed. Historically, the best attested of these ancient kingdoms was centred at *Al Cluith*, 'rock of the Clyde', or Dumbarton, 'fort of the Britons'. Its core territory of the Lennox embraced Loch Lomond and corresponded closely to the later county of Dunbartonshire. The other British kingdom north of the Clyde was Manaw, which was centred on Stirling and included much of the Forth valley.

In the Pictish cultural zone, which extended north of the Forth to Skye and the Northern Isles, there were a number of kingdoms, such as Atholl, Moray and Orkney, but apart from their names they have left little historical evidence. Amongst the Picts the most eminent kingdom was Fortriu, which included Strathearn and some of Strathmore. Linguistically the Britons and Picts were closely related, speaking tongues from the Brithonic language group (which includes Welsh).

In the ninth century these speakers of native British dialects shared the north with Gaelic speakers in the west and English speakers in the south-east. The Gaelic kingdom, approximately equivalent to modern Argyll, was called Dál Riata. In mythological tradition the Gaels came to Britain from Ireland in the sixth century at the same time that Germanic speakers from the Continent began to settle in Northumbria. These Anglo-Saxons established a new dynasty which was so successful that by the middle of the seventh century the British kingdoms of Gododdin (the Lothians) and Rheged (the south-west) had been conquered and significant English settlement took place in these regions.

Dupplin Cross
The west face contains the panel with the badly weathered inscription.
HISTORIC SCOTLAND/CROWN COPYRIGHT

A further complication to this ethno-linguistic situation was the arrival of Norse settlers in the Northern and Western Isles around the end of the eighth century. From these new settlements were launched devastating Viking raids, so fierce that they destabilised the political landscape. The most enduring consequence of this disruption was the collapse of the Pictish kingdom and its replacement by a Gaelic one in the former Pictish heartland. By the early 900s, Alba had secured its political future, but the kingdom of Dál Riata disappeared. The kingdom of Dumbarton was also replaced by a new hybrid Norse-British kingdom on the Clyde, known as Cumbria.

Further south the impact was, if anything, more severe. The kingdom of Northumbria collapsed during the ninth century, releasing the Lothians and the south-west. These were the first areas into which the new kings of Alba and Cumbria sought to extend their dominion. Territorial expansion by the post-Viking kingdoms thus becomes one of the main themes of these centuries.

The post-Viking kingdoms differed in significant ways from those that preceded them. Firstly, royal authority was greater. The rudiments of government began to appear in the form of royal officials and legal institutions. The clearest evidence of this change in the nature of kingship was the emergence of Scone as the ceremonial centre of Alba. This site of popular assembly became the place where the kings were publicly inaugurated, and in time came to signify the kingdom itself.

The post-Viking Age Church went through a similar process of institutional development. As the Church became wealthier, it became more powerful and more visible in secular politics. The tendency for sculpture of the tenth and eleventh centuries to be concentrated in a few well-endowed churches is one sign of this, but it is the growth in the saints' cults that provides the clearest indication of the increasing power of the leading churches.

Forteviot Neolithic Cropmarks
Aerial view of the henge monuments, associated enclosure and barrows in the foreground with Forteviot village in the distance (see transcription on page 36, caption).
RCAHMS

Forteviot Village Cropmarks

Cemetery of Pictish square barrows and simple Christian graves revealed from the air.

RCAHMS

The Dupplin Cross and Forteviot

Until recently, this cross stood on the Gask ridge overlooking the heart of Strathearn, but excavation has shown that this was not its original location. Probably it once stood near the church and cemetery of the royal palace of Forteviot. Its worn inscription refers to Custantin, son of Urguist (789?–820), one of the great Pictish kings. In its imagery the cross sums up the ideological basis of kingship at this time. Warriors of various grades are conspicuously represented, while the harpist evokes both King David of the Old Testament and a bardic presence in the court. Although there are none of the familiar Pictish symbols, the figures clearly draw upon the Pictish sculptural tradition.

This sculpture is the most revealing relic of what was the chief royal seat of the Gaelic kingdom: home to Cinaed mac Ailpín (843–58) and his brother. Seventeenth-century poetic tradition suggests that Malcolm III 'Canmore' lived here and charters of Malcolm IV (dated 1162–4) and of William I (dated 1165–71) show that it remained important into the twelfth century. Thereafter it drops off the royal circuit, but it remained a royal estate until the fourteenth century.

Part of the appeal of Forteviot appears to have been its ancient landscape setting. Aerial photographs record the presence of a remarkable set of cropmarks less than a kilometre south of Forteviot, all that remains of a previously unsuspected prehistoric ritual landscape. The cropmarks reveal a vast enclosure defined by large pits, which originally held massive timber posts. The most enduring features were the henge monuments marked out by broad banks and ditches, which like the pit-defined enclosure, date from the Neolithic period (3500–2000 BC). Alongside the monuments are slighter traces of burial mounds, some of which are square, the characteristic form of Pictish barrows. The Neolithic henges were substantial structures and must have been prominent local landmarks prior to the introduction of modern agricultural methods. The square barrows and the proximity to Forteviot make it plain that the Picts were attracted to the ancient religious centre.

Dupplin Cross

A mounted warrior stands over a row of soldiers on the east side.

HISTORIC SCOTLAND/CROWN COPYRIGHT

Natives and Newcomers

Although the political landscape of early medieval Scotland is imperfectly understood, the contours of the most important areas are relatively well-known. The core of the kingdom of Alba was located in the chief kingdom of former Pictland. Known from at least the eighth century as 'Fortriu', this certainly included western Perthshire (ie from Perth to Dunblane) and may have extended as far east as Forfar. From the loose way that contemporary records refer to the 'King of the Picts' and the 'King of Fortriu', it appears that the King of Fortriu was usually the chief king south of the Grampians. Elsewhere in Pictland our knowledge is fuzzier.

The southern Pictish kings ruled over some of the richest land in Scotland; they controlled their territory through a network of estates. The most spectacular of these were centred at fortified hilltops such as Dundurn, but also included old Roman fortifications at Bertha by the Tay (known as 'Rathiveralmond', the *rath* or fortified enclosure at the mouth of the River Almond) and unenclosed places like Forteviot. From an archaeological perspective the best known of these sites is Dundurn, at the head of Strathearn, controlling the key land route between Pictland and Dál Riata. Dundurn was built following the Iron Age fort-building tradition. Its ramparts and buildings were made of unmortared masonry, stabilised by a nailed timber-frame. On the summit stood a thick-walled fortified building, a substantial dwelling, or possibly a great hall. This was surrounded by a series of fortified terraces, which accommodated other members of the household and provided areas for work and storage. Like their counterparts in Argyll and the south-west, such as Dunadd and Mote of Mark, the inhabitants of Dundurn enjoyed pottery and glassware imported from the Continent and supported a high-class metalworking industry on-site.

Moncrieff Hill, with its remarkable hillfort, appears to have been the principal political centre of Fortriu. The place-name, which means 'hill of the tree', is believed to refer to a conspicuous 'tribal' tree. Within the wider Gaelic world, sacred trees often

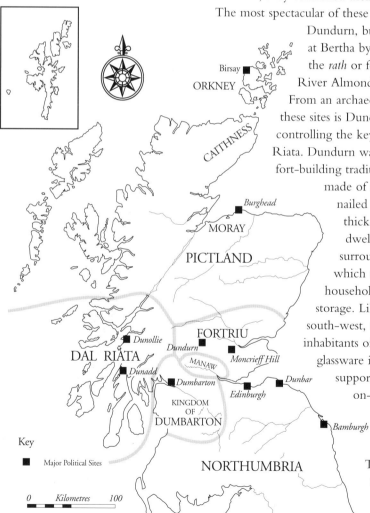

Key

■ Major Political Sites

0   Kilometres   100

Dundurn Glass Boss
A virtuoso example of the glass maker's art which combines black, white and blue shoe.

(*Above*)
Dundurn Hillfort
The hill rises up from the valley bottom at the head of Strathearn. The terraces leading up to the summit are clearly visible.
STEPHEN T. DRISCOLL

(*Below*)
Moncrieff Hill
View from the south of the craggy ridge crowned by the hillfort, on the left above the tree line.
STEPHEN T. DRISCOLL

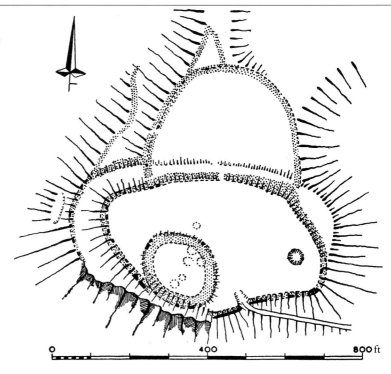

Plan of Moncrieff Hillfort
The various ramparts show that the hill was repeatedly fortified. The large enclosure includes a massive artificial pool or well.
RCHAMS

marked places of assembly and royal inauguration. The hill is a great landmark; it dominates the confluence of the Earn and the Tay. Although unexcavated and therefore less well-understood than Dundurn, the summit is crowned with an impressive complex of stone-built ramparts and includes a large artificial well or pond. Its political importance is suggested by the record of a battle, which took place there in 729 between rivals for the Pictish throne.

The ecclesiastical centre of Fortriu was at Abernethy, a monastery endowed by Pictish kings around 625. It was eventually eclipsed by St Andrews, but not before it had accumulated extensive estates.

The eastern extension of the Grampian massif which runs almost to the North Sea coast at Stonehaven, known from early times as the Mounth, was a formidable barrier. The lands north of the Mounth were always difficult to rule for kings based on the Tay, and prior to the tenth century Moray was independent. The formidable stronghold of Dunottar guarding the east end of the Mounth was the most northerly site held by the kings of Alba before the 1000s. Within Moray the most conspicuous political centre was the great promontory fort of Burghead, built in early Pictish times using timber-framed ramparts (see *Surviving in Symbols*, this series). This largest of Pictish fortifications is celebrated for its panels of finely carved bulls, but its deep rock-cut well is just as important as an indicator of its ritual or ceremonial significance.

Ecclesiastical centres in Moray are easier to identify than secular centres because their characteristic sculpture can be dated with more accuracy than dry-stone walls. Kineddar, Birnie and Spynie appear to have been the principal churches before the establishment of the cathedral at Elgin in 1224. Mortlach, in Dufftown, appears to have been the pre-eminent church in the Spey valley, while in Buchan the most important church we know of was at Deer. Although little is known about Buchan as a whole in this period, a unique illuminated gospel book from Deer does survive (see page 51).

As one moves further north it is possible to identify local centres of importance, usually by the presence of sculpture, as at Golspie in Sutherland, but there is no substitute for excavated evidence as can be seen at the Brough of Birsay on Orkney. Here sagas and other sources link the tidal island with the earls of Orkney and identify it both as a secular centre of power and as an important church associated with the cult of St Magnus. A series of excavations there have revealed that the below the Norse levels there are structures, monumental sculptures and fine metalworking debris of a Pictish date. It is clear that Birsay began as the seat of a Pictish magnate.

Kineddar Lion
This fragment of a lively lion indicates the quality of the sculpture which once graced the important religious centre in Moray.
TOM GRAY

Dunottar Castle

The peninsula to the south of Stonehaven is virtually an island. Its summit is covered by medieval and later structures, which obscure any traces of earlier activity. It is ideally positioned to monitor movement through the narrow gap between the Mounth and the sea.

HISTORIC SCOTLAND/CROWN COPYRIGHT

Burghead

This aerial photograph reveals the majesty of the great fortified headland, which is largely masked by the early nineteenth-century town. Without doubt it was the chief centre on the Moray coast.

IAN RALSTON

Brough of Birsay, Orkney
Aerial view which emphasises the twelfth-century church at the core of the jarl's palace, which overlies the Pictish power centre. Surrounding this are numerous dwellings capable of housing an impressive household.
HISTORIC SCOTLAND/CROWN COPYRIGHT

Birsay Symbol Stone
Probably the most evocative indication of the importance of Birsay in Pictish times is this slab with a representation of three warriors. The superior status of the foremost is clearly indicated in the detail of dress, weapons and hairstyle.
NATIONAL MUSEUM OF SCOTLAND

Gaelic expansion

The Scots located their homeland in Argyll because it was here that the kings of Dál Riata emerged in the sixth century. Throughout the Middle Ages this Gaelic-speaking district was believed to have been created by Irish colonisation. However, there are good reasons why we should regard the Scots of Dál Riata as essentially Gaelic-speaking people of local British origin (see *Saints and Sea-kings,* this series). Periodically during the Middle Ages, this linguistic community was also a political entity which spanned the North Channel, most recently when Antrim was subject to the Lords of the Isles. The depth of the Gaelic linguistic identity is an indication of a deep cultural continuity, which is evident in the Irish royal ancestry of the kings of Dál Riata, in the origin legends linking their *Lia Fail* ('Stone of Destiny') to Tara, and in their chief saints who were also widely venerated in Ireland, particularly Columba.

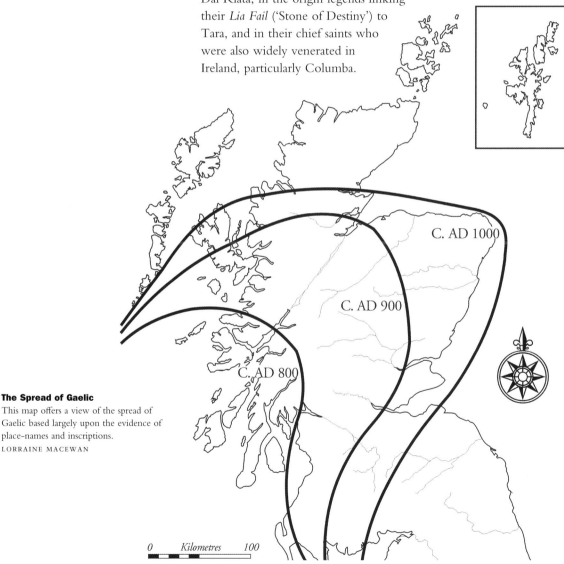

The Spread of Gaelic

This map offers a view of the spread of Gaelic based largely upon the evidence of place-names and inscriptions.

LORRAINE MACEWAN

Nurturing the monastic community of Columba was probably the most important cultural and political contribution made to Scotland by Dál Riata. During the seventh and eighth centuries, while the fortunes of the secular rulers fluctuated wildly, Iona developed into the most important Christian centre in northern Britain. Arguably, it was this religious authority, above all, which encouraged the spread of the Gaelic language eastwards as far as Fife and Buchan. The degree of the cultural transformation is best indicated by the widespread adoption of Gaelic in place-names, which reveals that a profound transformation in the cultural identity of the land-owning classes occurred in the ninth to tenth century.

The adoption of Gaelic language and culture characterises social and political life in Scotland from the ninth to the twelfth century, but the rise in prominence of the language did not ensure the continuing importance of the old power centres of Dál Riata. The great fortress of Dunadd disappears from the historical record after the eighth century, and the treasures of Iona, including the relics of Columba, were dispersed to Dunkeld in Perthshire and Kells in Ireland in 848 or 849. At the same time Argyll became a backwater until after the Viking Age, when a new Kingdom of the Isles, ruled by the descendants of hybrid Gaelic-Norse Vikings, took shape in the twelfth century. A degree of political continuity from pre-Viking times is suggested by the selection of ancient strongholds as the sites of new castles of the twelfth and thirteenth centuries, as at Castle Tioram.

Lost British kingdoms

The most overlooked peoples of the area that was to become Scotland are those who originally occupied the southern half of the modern country – the Lothians, the Forth valley, Strathclyde and the south-west. The most important centre of the northern Britons was Dumbarton, which ruled over a kingdom running from the mouth of the Clyde to the headwaters of the Kelvin in the Lennox. The other northern British kingdoms are much less well-known, because they were conquered early by the Angles and incorporated into Greater Northumbria (see *Angels, Fools and Tyrants*, this series). The principal seat of the Gododdin who ruled the Lothians was at *Din Eydin*, Edinburgh. It was conquered in 638. Manaw, the kingdom based in the Forth valley and centred at Stirling, became the frontier of the Anglian expansion north.

Anglian Whithorn
Archaeological excavations have inspired this reconstruction of a massive well-ordered monastery on the eve of the Viking Age.
DAVE POLLOCK/WHITHORN
ARCHAEOLOGICAL TRUST

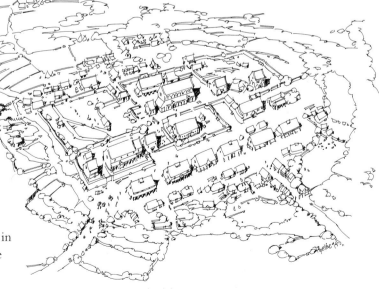

Iona Abbey

The restored Benedictine abbey occupies the site established by Columba which is separated from Mull by a narrow channel.
HISTORIC SCOTLAND/CROWN COPYRIGHT

Castle Tioram, Moidart

The medieval castle stands upon a tidal island occupied since at least the seventh century. It commands one of the most strategically vital points north of Ardnamurchan.
GLASGOW UNIVERSITY

All three kingdoms in central Scotland had at their political heart a fortification built in a place of great natural strength and prominence. However, there was no such landmark to indicate the importance of Whithorn in Galloway, but here, outside one of the great religious centres of the north, flourished one of the richest trading centres known to archaeologists. There is abundant evidence for regular trade with the Continent from the seventh century. The combination of a pilgrimage centre with a flourishing port evidently made Whithorn irresistible to the Northumbrians, who had annexed the region by the early 700s, and who greatly expanded the monastery at its centre. In all of these places, it is possible to discern the British political landscape beneath the later overlay of Anglian settlement. The chief places of the British retained their importance although some of their names were translated into English, like Edinburgh and Whithorn.

The one British kingdom to survive until the twelfth century was in Strathclyde. Although Dumbarton itself was ruined in the Viking wars, a British presence persisted on the Clyde centred at Govan. The clearest evidence of this former period of greatness is found in Govan Old Parish Church, which occupies a raised, oval enclosure that has protected it from encroachment by the shipyards and tenements. The church houses Scotland's third largest collection of early medieval sculpture, testimony to its political and religious importance during the 900s and 1000s. Govan was a large, wealthy parish, which, exceptionally, ran across a major river to include the royal seat of Partick on the north bank of the Clyde. Latterly, this kingdom was known as Cumbria, but very little contemporary historical evidence survives, partially because Govan lost its position, and presumably much of its patronage, when Glasgow was selected as the new seat for the Bishop of Cumbria in the early 1100s, but we may also suspect that the Gaelic-speaking élite were not much interested in the British past.

The expansion and contraction of Northumbria

English has been spoken in the south-east of Scotland since the sixth century, when the Anglian kings of Northumbria began a period of aggressive expansion. At its peak, Northumbrian rule extended into Pictland beyond the Tay and over British territories as far north-west as Kyle and Carrick. Of all the Anglo-Saxon kingdoms, Northumbria was the most British. The English settlement was less dense and there appears to have been a high level of accommodation and adoption of British structures. Almost all of the important places in Northumbria began as British centres, as at Dunbar and Whithorn, where recent excavations have documented the transition. Both places saw

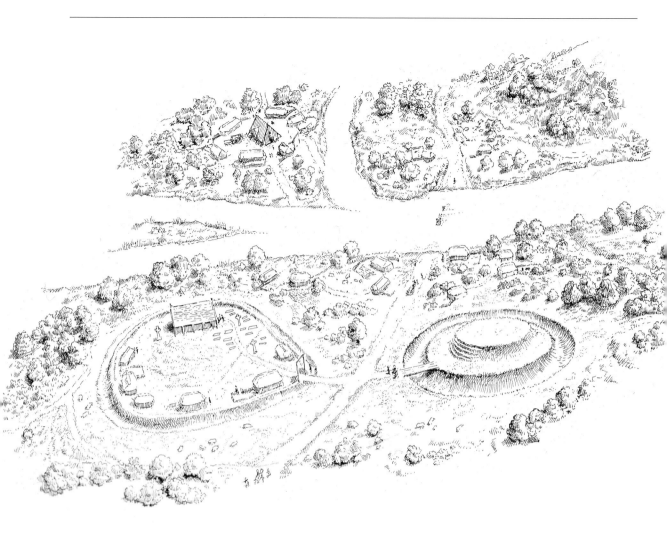

View of Govan and Partick *c.* AD 1000
Reconstruction of Govan Old Parish
Church and the Doomster Hill on the
south bank of the Clyde looking north to
the royal estate of Partick.
CHRIS BROWN

wholesale rebuilding following newly developed architectural styles,
which combined Continental forms with native British traditions, and
in the process became politically more important.

One consequence of the Viking wars which destroyed
Northumbria as a political entity was that the Anglian kings lost
control of the Borders and the south-west. By 973 the Scottish king's
rule extended south of the Tyne, while the kingdom of Cumbria,
centred around Govan, extended south of the Solway. Nevertheless,
the three centuries of Anglian influence had long-lasting
consequences. Archaeologists and art-historians tend to point to the
presence of ecclesiastical sculpture as the most visible sign of the
Northumbrian presence. Linguistic historians draw attention to
place-names, like Athelstaneford (East Lothian) or Kirkcudbright
(from Cuthbert's kirk) as evidence of widespread settlement.
However, possibly the most important contributions of the English
were the almost invisible, institutional innovations relating to the

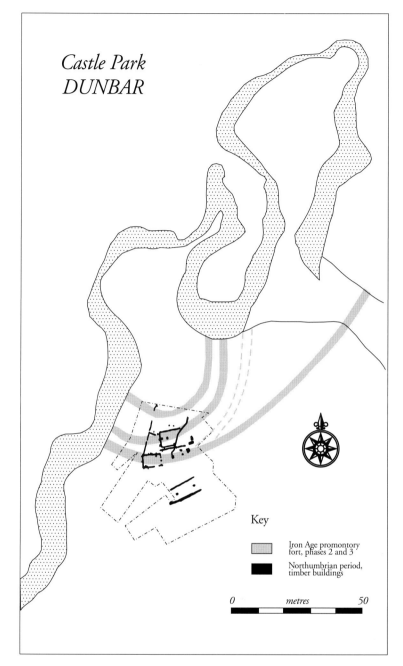

Castle Park
DUNBAR

Key

Iron Age promontory
fort, phases 2 and 3

Northumbrian period,
timber buildings

0   *metres*   50

Dunbar, East Lothian
This British stronghold was adopted by the
incoming Anglians. The Iron Age ramparts
were filled in and new buildings
superimposed upon them.
LORRAINE MACEWAN

practice of land management and government administration. The
carve-up of the landscape into shires, the appointment of royal
officials, and, perhaps, the introduction of territorial parishes are first
recognised historically when the English terms *shire* and *thane* appear.
Underpinning these institutions were practices of estate management,
the exploitation of landed resources, and the mustering of men which
became the foundation of the kingdom of the Scots of the twelfth
century.

Govan and the kings of the Clyde

The meaning of the name Govan is disputed, but it probably derives from the Brittonic *gwo-/go-*, 'small' and *ban*, 'hill', which is thought to refer to the now demolished artificial mound known as the Doomster Hill. An eighteenth-century engraving shows it as a flat-topped mound, with a wide step halfway up, towering over contemporary cottages near the ford over the Clyde. Measurements of the artificial mound made before it was demolished to make way for a shipyard in the late nineteenth century recorded that it was about 45 metres in diameter and stood about 5 metres high. Although there is no contemporary evidence, antiquarian tradition suggests that the Doomster Hill was a moot hill or court hill. If so, this was of great political significance as the place where the king came before his subjects and exercised his legal authority. The stepped form can be paralleled at moot hills at two other major Viking Age centres: the Tynwald on the Isle of Man and the Thingmote ('Assembly moot [hill]') of Dublin.

Small-scale archaeological excavations at Govan Old Parish Church have demonstrated that the pear shape of the enclosure is ancient and that the elevation of the churchyard was caused by the rising ground level within the original bank and ditch boundary. Radiocarbon dates show that the boundary was dug no later than the ninth century. The site of the early medieval church has also been identified to the east of the modern church along with traces of a very early Christian cemetery going back to the fifth century. Excavations have also exposed a road from the east, which linked the original entrance to the churchyard with the Doomster Hill.

The forty-seven pieces of sculpture known from Govan, most of which are massive gravestones of the tenth and eleventh centuries, are strongly suggestive of royal patronage. There are four monumental crosses, a strong sign that it was a major church. The oldest gravestones, the so-called hogbacks, are a type of house-shaped monument found only in those areas of Norse settlement in northern England and southern Scotland. The Govan hogbacks are the largest known examples and are dated to about AD 900. While the collection of cross-inscribed gravestones is by far the largest in Scotland, without question the most impressive sculpture is the monolithic sarcophagus, which is decorated with interlace panels and features a mounted warrior at the hunt. The sarcophagus is widely considered to be the finest example of British sculpture and its imagery invites a royal interpretation.

In the absence of historical records relating to the period of Govan's prominence, interpretation of the site's significance rests upon the archaeological evidence and later historical associations. Given the abundance of sculpture and the Doomster Hill, it suggests that Govan was the political centre of the kingdom in the centuries following the demise of Dumbarton (sacked in 870) and the rise of Glasgow Cathedral (founded 1114–18). Twelfth-century sources indicate that Partick was an estate of the royal house of Strathclyde, which provides a political context and source of patronage for this extraordinary collection. The character of the early sculpture and the form of the moot hill both indicate Norse influence and it is not unreasonable to suppose that there was a significant Scandinavian presence in the court.

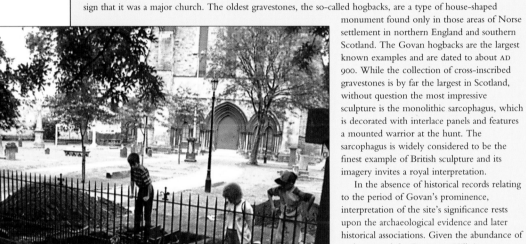

Digging at Govan Old Parish Church
The excavations of the 1990s produced evidence showing that the site was centuries older than was suggested by the sculpture. Here the soiling filling the boundary ditch (the *vallum*) is being removed.
GLASGOW UNIVERSITY

Govan Hogback

The earliest sculpture at Govan dates to *c.* AD 900 and is a distinctly Norse form of burial monument in the shape of a house or perhaps a church.
HISTORIC SCOTLAND/CROWN COPYRIGHT

The Govan Sarcophagus

This unique monolithic sarcophagus is the most impressive piece of sculpture from Govan and it is hard to resist the idea that it was made for a king.
HISTORIC SCOTLAND/CROWN COPYRIGHT

Govan in 1758 by Robert Paul

This view by Robert Paul was made from the north side of the Clyde. The Doomster Hill stands to the left of the ferry landing and only the bell tower of Govan Old Parish Church is visible amongst the trees on the right.
GLASGOW CITY LIBRARIES

Viking Age Dynamics

Scandinavian Settlement

The area of settlement in the north and west provided a secure platform for Viking raids on vulnerable coastal monasteries and assaults on the rich heartlands of northern Britain.

LORRAINE MACEWAN

Colonies of raiders and traders

Whatever the direct effect of Viking raiding, the Norse were at the centre of the violent social and political upheavals of the ninth and tenth centuries. The impact of the wars of the Viking Age was most apparent in the political and cultural centres, which had the most to lose. For the great monasteries, the Viking Age was the worst of times, when, because of repeated plunderings, literary and artistic activity diminished. As a result of this assault on the centres of learning, the Viking Age is historically darker than the preceding centuries. Only the raids and battles

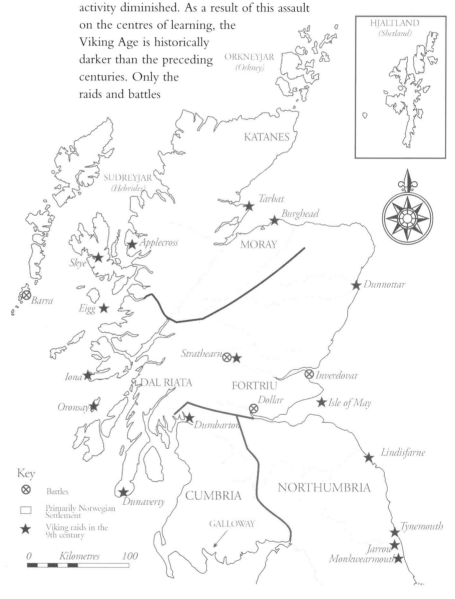

stand out in written history. Initially the paganism of the Vikings set them apart, but even several centuries after their settlement and conversion to Christianity their descendants continued to speak a Norse dialect and remained politically part of the Norse world.

At the dawn of the Viking Age a hunger for land motivated substantial numbers of Norse to brave the North Sea in search of more attractive farmlands among the islands of the North Atlantic. Scandinavian seafarers became common visitors to the British Isles around 800, and during the course of the following centuries they colonised substantial areas of Scotland, northern England and Ireland (see *The Sea Road*, this series). The density of Norse place-names in the Northern and Western Isles is testimony to the success of these adventurers and the attractiveness of the islands. Their island settlements were ideal bases from which to mount pirate raids, in which they used the tactical advantage of their superior ships to full effect. During the course of the ninth century the pattern of plundering developed from lightning smash-and-grab raids on vulnerable monasteries to sustained campaigns of extortion and conquest. In a short period their military might established the Vikings as masters of the Irish Sea and they set about the construction of permanent kingdoms. Temporary refuges were transformed into harbours with important permanent trading centres. Dublin was the greatest of the urban Viking foundations, drawing upon the wealth of the Irish East Midlands. Controlling the Irish Sea, however, was not sufficient for the powerful and ambitious Dublin Vikings and during the ninth and tenth centuries they repeatedly sought to extend their dominion over Yorkshire and southern Northumbria, with some success.

Viking Age Whithorn

A reconstruction based on well-preserved waterlogged remains of structures similar to those known from Dublin.
DAVE POLLOCK/WHITHORN
ARCHAEOLOGICAL TRUST

The Norse Irish Sea

The Norse naval superiority in the Irish Sea had important consequences for Scotland. The kingdom of Dál Riata disappeared from the historical record after its king was killed fighting alongside the Picts against the Vikings in 839. It is widely believed that Dál Riata was succeeded by a hybrid Gaelic-Norse society in Argyll and the Hebrides. Certainly several key medieval Gaelic kindreds traced their roots to Scandinavian leaders: the MacSweens from the Norse *Svein*, Fergus of Galloway, and most famously Somerled from the Norse 'summer voyager'. From the security of the Isles, pirates of mixed culture and descent operated

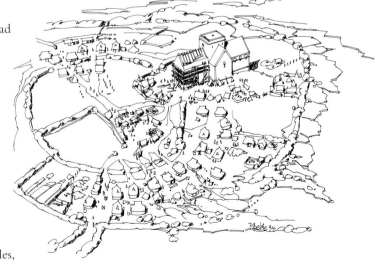

unchecked. The greatest of the islands ruled by Vikings was Man, ideally positioned to dominate the Irish Sea, the Solway Firth and the Clyde estuary.

The west was not the only source of Viking trouble; large Viking armies terrorised northern and central England, leaving political instability in their wake. The most spectacular casualty was the kingdom of Northumbria, which collapsed completely after the Battle of Brunanburh in 937 (see page 60). This created a power vacuum which would prove irresistible to generations of Dublin Vikings. Although not subject to such sustained assaults as Northumbria, the Pictish heartlands also attracted

the periodic attentions of Viking armies. The crushing defeats suffered by the men of Fortriu in 839 appear to have brought down the old Pictish order and opened the way for Cinaed mac Ailpín to seize the kingship of the southern Picts. Further Viking raids in the Pictish heartlands in the 860s and 870s may explain why so little is known of Cinaed's successors.

The ambition to construct a single Viking kingdom based on York and Dublin, though never fully achieved, had a profound impact on the wider political landscape of northern Britain. Probably the most spectacular casualty of these ambitions was Dumbarton, which was attacked by a formidable army led by the Dublin Vikings in 870. After a four-month-long siege, the fortress was overcome and utterly destroyed, exposing Clydesdale to extensive plundering. The following year it is reported that 200 ships were needed to transport slaves to the Dublin market. After its sack, Dumbarton descended into four centuries of historical obscurity.

The Sack of Dumbarton
In AD 870 Vikings from Dublin toppled mighty Dumbarton after a four-month-long siege. The result was catastrophic and led to the extensive seizure of slaves.
CHRIS BROWN

Long-term consequences

The Viking predations caused nothing less than the remaking of the political landscape. None of the kingdoms from the eighth century emerged unchanged and most disappeared forever. On the Scottish periphery, the Vikings built a series of island-based lordships in Orkney, the Hebrides and Man. In Orkney, the native Picts were swept away and, although there was a degree of continuity to the political landscape, the new Jarls (earls) came under the active overlordship of the Norwegian king. Norway was too far away to allow the king to exercise as much control over the kingdom of Man, which at the end of the Viking Age was the most powerful Norse kingdom. In the Hebrides, a Gaelic-Norse Kingdom of the Isles wrested its independence from overlordship from Man, but remained nominally subject to Norway.

The destruction of Dumbarton led to a new configuration of political power on the Clyde. The centre of power shifted upstream to Govan, which became the centre of the kingdom of Cumbria. This new British kingdom was ruled by an ethnically diverse élite, which also exhibited strong Norse and Gaelic influences, clearly reflecting the ascendancy of the lords of Argyll and the western seas. Although not as dense as in the Scottish isles, there was considerable Norse settlement around the Solway. Remarkably Whithorn remained an important commercial centre, but remodelled itself as a Viking trading centre, introducing building forms and producing goods, such as bone combs, which are typical of Viking York and Dublin.

The kingdom of the southern Picts was unusual in that it survived more or less intact, but not unaltered. A Gaelic kingdom was constructed upon the Pictish framework. This Gaelic ascendancy, linked to the career of Cinaed mac Ailpín, developed new forms of royal authority to cope with the changing political realities of the Viking Age. In time, the name of the kingdom was altered to Alba to reflect the new political reality.

Viking Combs from Whithorn

Some of the clearest evidence for the development of a Viking type of trading and manufacturing centre consists of the debris from the making of combs.

WHITHORN ARCHAEOLOGICAL TRUST

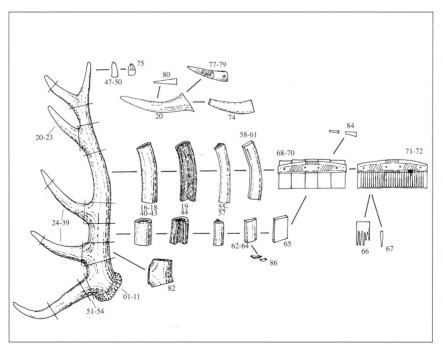

Picts into Scots:
the Growth of Gaelic Royal Power

Conventionally, the coming together of the Picts and Scots under the rule of Cinaed mac Ailpín has been seen as a ninth-century union of the crowns comparable to that in 1603 between Scotland and England. Because even now it is not entirely clear how Gaelic came to extinguish Pictish language and culture in the east, this comfortable vision of a union of equals has proved a popular myth. The Gaelic-speaking Scots were the minority, however, and the conquest of the Picts must have involved some violence. In some ways, the most interesting point is the degree to which Pictish institutions persisted, even as the Pictish language disappeared.

Nowhere is this clearer than when looking at the kingship. The leading kings of southern Pictland ruled Fortriu, a kingdom centred on Forteviot, 9 kilometres west of Perth. Although there were many other royal centres, Forteviot was evidently the most important. Cinaed mac Ailpín ruled from there and when he died here in 858 he was described as 'king of the Picts'. It seems likely that Cinaed would have been bilingual and that his followers included Scots and Picts. Indeed, his immediate successors were also known as 'kings of the Picts' until around 900, when the new term for this Gaelic kingdom, Alba, was adopted.

Behind this royal stability, Gaelic language was spreading east in the ninth century and people with it. This process of population displacement at a high social level is documented in a group of place-names characteristic of Pictland.

The Extent of Alba
The distribution of pit- place-names, such as Pitlochry, indicates where former Pictish estates were taken over by Gaels. The pit-element is Pictish, but 90 per cent of the places have Gaelic second elements.
LORRAINE MACEWAN

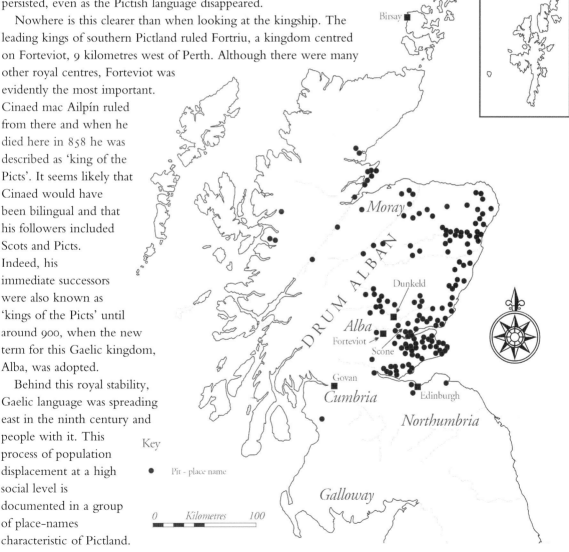

Key

● Pit - place name

0   Kilometres   100

The Apostle Stone from Dunkeld
A rare depiction of a new testament scene on the base of a Scottish high cross. Such images are much more typical of the sculpture on Irish high crosses.
HISTORIC SCOTLAND/CROWN COPYRIGHT

The Forteviot Arch
Remarkable evidence for a masonry church within the royal palace complex, which is unique in northern Britain.
NATIONAL MUSEUMS OF SCOTLAND

Places containing the element *pit-* are found in the most attractive agricultural land and probably represent Pictish estates, many of which are occupied still by substantial farms. While *pit-* is undoubtedly Pictish for 'piece or parcel', in place-names it is almost always coupled with a Gaelic second element, most commonly a personal name. The apparent lesson here is that certain attractive Pictish estates were taken over lock, stock and barrel by Gaelic speakers, or, at least, by people with Gaelic names. There was therefore a Gaelic aristocratic ascendancy. Given the context of the Viking wars, this ascendancy is likely to have been built on military achievement. The success of Cinaed mac Ailpín and his kindred, the Cenél nGabráin, seems to have been a case in point. But there was also a cultural aspect to this. The Gaelic cultural ascendancy was encouraged by the Gaelic-speaking clergy associated with the cult of Columba.

The Gaelic presence in the east was not newly introduced in the ninth century but extends back as far as the sixth century when the first Irish monks were reported in northern Britain. Already by the 730s there was enough Gaelic spoken east of the mountains known as Drum Alban, 'the spine of Britain' (ie the Grampians), that the name Atholl, believed to mean 'new Ireland', was coined. If the spread of Gaelic was intimately linked with the prestige of the community of Iona, then it can be best appreciated in the spread of the cult of Columba. In the seventh century, Iona constructed a network of monasteries which stretched from Lindisfarne in Northumbria to Durrow in Ireland. In the centuries before Rome exerted any real control over the Church, the 'family' of Columba was perhaps the most influential Christian organisation in the British Isles. Its spiritual leadership was reinforced by powerful secular associations, most

importantly as the patron saint of the Cenél nGabráin. In 848/9 Columba was elevated to the premier position among the Scottish saints by Cinaed, who had some of Columba's relics brought to Dunkeld which he made the chief church in his kingdom. Apart from sculpture, nothing of this church survives.

St Vigean's Church, Angus
The modern church occupies a steep sided knoll towering over the village which surrounds it.
KATHERINE FORSYTH

Seats of authority

Forteviot is not remarkable simply because Cinaed mac Ailpín lived and died there; it represents a milestone in the development of the Scottish kingship. Unlike all of the other named places occupied by early medieval kings, Forteviot was not a fortress, it was a 'palace'. It is so called in the contemporary record of Cinaed's death, but what is meant by 'palace'? The situation of Forteviot is not defensive and there are no traces of any fortified enclosure. On the other hand, there is evidence for artistic and architectural patronage on an impressive scale. The most splendid piece of sculpture is the Dupplin Cross (see pages 6, 10–11, 13), but there are other fragments including a unique arch. This arch seems most likely to represent the chancel arch of a royal church from within the palace complex. The find-spot of the arch in the Water of May, which runs through Forteviot, suggests that the church may have stood originally on an isolated hillock, as the church of St Vigean's in Angus does still. Aerial photographs show that Forteviot was the site of a major cemetery,

Transcription of the Forteviot Cropmark Complex

Immediately to the south of the modern village is one of the most spectacular concentrations of prehistoric ritual monuments in eastern Scotland. Chief amongst these cropmarks is a group of Neolithic henge monuments (13–16), associated with barrows, including ones of Pictish date (18–20). Closer to the village and east of the church, cropmarks suggest the presence of a cemetery consisting of simple graves (C and D) and Pictish barrows (4–9).

RCAHMS

COMPUTER PLOT FROM AERIAL PHOTOGRAPHS
USE ONLY WITH CAUTION. COPYRIGHT RCAHMS

which included burials in characteristic Pictish square barrows. We can only guess at the rest of the layout, but it would seem that the term 'palace' was used to signal that Forteviot was the seat of a great king, not the stronghold of a mere warlord.

Forteviot then seems to mark the point where the rhetoric of power had shifted away from the naked display of military strength, as for instance in the fort at Dundurn, to power as seen in the command of resources and architectural expertise. If we have to guess, then the palaces of Carolingian France may have provided the ultimate inspiration.

It was not just in Pictland that power shifted away from the hillforts; the British royal centre that developed at Govan and Partick after the sack of Dumbarton in 870 shares a number of common features. Partick, the royal seat, does not occupy a position with any defensive capabilities on the opposite bank of the Clyde from the church of Govan. At Govan the most likely explanation for the dozens of gravestones of the tenth and eleventh centuries is that it too was home to a powerful dynasty.

Ceremonial centres

Forteviot is exceptional in another way. The most spectacular concentration of prehistoric ritual monuments in eastern Scotland occupies the fields to the south of the village. It would seem that proximity to these sites, which were already ancient in the ninth century, was an important aspect of Forteviot's setting. Although the Picts can have had no scientific appreciation of the age of these monuments, the most impressive of which date to the Neolithic (about 2500 BC), it seems entirely likely that the monuments did hold some sort of ancestral aura. They must have contributed some ancient legitimacy to the place and the activities which occurred there.

One strong possibility is that these monuments served as the focal points for popular assembly. No traditions survive to suggest how they were used by the Picts. What is clear, however, is that by the end of the ninth century, as the kingdom of Alba was taking shape, certain prominent places of popular assembly were being constructed which had a strong association with the exercise of royal authority. Chief amongst these was of course the Moot Hill at Scone, but the Doomster Hill at Govan was probably taking shape at this time too. Many minor moot hills are known throughout Scotland, some of which made use of existing prehistoric burial mounds, and all of which may be seen as part of wider change in the exercise of legal rule.

The appearance of Scone as a royal assembly place can be precisely dated to 906 by an entry in the *Chronicle of the Kings of Alba*:

'And in his sixth year King Constantine [II son of Áed] and Bishop Cellach vowed together with the Gaels [*Scotti*], to maintain the laws and disciplines of the faith and the rights of churches and of gospel-books on the Hill of Faith close to the royal *civitas* of Scone.'

The stress in this near contemporary account is laid on the public proclamation of the law and on ecclesiastical authority, but we can see here the origins of the popular acclamation of kings at Scone. By 906, Constantine had ruled for some six years, but for most of this time he had been engaged in prolonged, and ultimately successful, campaigns against the Vikings. The decision to elevate Scone to ceremonial centre of the kingdom appears to be linked to the change in name to Alba. It may well be that the Moot Hill at Scone was built at this time. Scone occupies a pivotal geographic position in the heart of southern Pictland, and, like Forteviot, Scone lay within an impressive ancient monumental landscape, which survives as cropmarks.

Thus we see that in the course of the ninth century the Gaelic kings developed the idea of the unfortified, palatial royal centre. They developed a ceremonial centre at which the full legal authority of the king could be exercised and they forged ever stronger links with the Church. In fact, the Church was fully integrated into the physical and conceptual arrangements of kingship.

Scone and Stone of Destiny

Scone is the traditional inaugural place of the kings of Scots and the original home of the Stone of Destiny. It lies in the Gowrie at a natural crossroads on the eastern bank of the Tay opposite Perth, at the upper tidal limit and the lowest fording place. The royal inaugural ceremonies were held on an artificial flat-topped mound known as the Moot Hill, which stands on a river terrace with wide prospects to the west over the Tay. On the slopes to the north, overlooking Scone, are the extensive prehistoric barrows and monuments at Blairhall.

Scone appears to have come to prominence only in the tenth century. There is no evidence for earlier Pictish royal activity there and the name itself is Gaelic. The mound is now within the policies of Scone Palace, where Alexander I established an Augustinian monastery *c.*1120. Apart from the Moot Hill, which is an large, low, oval mound (*c.*90 metres by 50 metres) standing 2–3 metres high, there is little evidence of the medieval ceremonial arrangements.

The Stone of Destiny is a block of Old Red Sandstone, which geological evidence indicates comes from an outcrop somewhere nearby. It may have begun life in some Roman or early Christian building, but has been reworked on several occasions. At some point, two large iron rings have been fastened to it for ease of handling. The royal candidate was seated upon the stone during the inauguration ceremony. The concept of a particular stone conferring legitimacy on royal inaugurations is a well-established feature of Irish royal inaugurations, which may have been introduced by the kings of Alba who claimed descent from Irish stock and believed that the stone originally came from Tara in Ireland.

In the fourteenth century the Stone of Destiny was removed by Edward I to Westminster, where it was incorporated into a throne which has been used in the coronation of English and subsequently British monarchs to the present day. The Stone was returned to Scotland in 1996.

The Stone of Destiny

The Moot Hill, Scone
The large flat mound stands only a couple of metres above ground level, but this would have provided a suitable stage for royal ceremonies. The building is part of a post-Reformation church.
HISTORIC SCOTLAND/CROWN COPYRIGHT

Constantine II at Scone in AD 906
The first mention of Scone describes a great assembly presided over by the king surrounded by his supporters and in the shadow of the ancient church.
CHRIS BROWN

The Church Matures: Old Traditions, New Influences

Christianity was first brought to Scotland in the fifth century and by the seventh century the missionary work seems to have been largely completed. The earliest Christian inscriptions found in the south of the country date to the fifth century (see *Angels, Fools and Heroes*, this series). Radiocarbon dates from cemeteries at Govan Old Parish Church, at the Catstane, Kirkliston (Lothian), and Hallowhill, St Andrews, indicate that by the end of the fifth century Christian burial practices were prevalent in the Scottish midlands. The peoples of the Hebrides were already Christian when Columba established Iona in 563.

Almost nothing is known of the earliest missionary phase. Only scraps of historical traditions are attached to the leading British and Pictish saints (see map on page 9): Ninian of Whithorn (died around 550), Kentigern of Glasgow (died in 612), Serf of Culross (died around 700), Curetan of Rosemarkie (died about 710). Only Columba (521–97) and Cuthbert (about 633–87) have anything like complete biographies, which is a measure of their popularity.

The position of the earliest churches was precarious, because they were dependent upon secular patronage. In Scotland, as elsewhere, the fledging churches were tied to the local political networks and over the long term a church's fate was determined by the fortunes of its patrons.

The old Pictish Church

Nowhere are the changes in political fortune more easily observed than at Abernethy, on the Tay. This monastery was founded by followers of St Brigit of Kildare in around 625 at the invitation of the Pictish king, who made it the principal church in Fortriu. Today, Abernethy churchyard is hardly imposing, but it is just possible to trace the concentric plan of the monastery in the street and its remarkable round tower remains the tallest building by far in the village. No complete sculpture survives, but the numerous fragments found reused as building stone in and around the village testify to its former status. The simple round tower dates to the eleventh or twelfth century, just about the time that Abernethy was being eclipsed by St Andrews. It is one of only two Irish-type round towers to survive in Scotland (the other is at Brechin). The battered collection of sculpture gives a poor impression of the importance of the place. Only its tower and its huge portfolio of estates and dependant churches strung along the southern shore of the lower Tay give a real impression of the economic and political power the abbots had.

The church at St Andrews was also the beneficiary of royal patronage. Although apparently dedicated to the obscure St Rule, the prestige attached to the relics of the apostle Andrew was eventually recognised as being more significant. The remains of saints and objects associated with them, known collectively as relics, were highly valued and much sought after because physical contact with these objects was believed to secure the saints' protection and blessings. The value of relics can be best appreciated through the precious metal and jewelled containers (reliquaries) fashioned to enhanced their visual appeal (see pages 46 and 69).

The most tangible evidence of Pictish patronage is the so-called St Andrews' sarcophagus, which is more accurately described as a stone shrine. This masterpiece of medieval Scottish sculpture was probably carved around 800 or a little earlier. The 'sarcophagus' consists of a set of stone panels which slot into carved posts to form a large box similar to those used to house relics. Its original function is uncertain; it was certainly intended as a piece of church furniture and may have been

Abernethy Tower
This is one of only two round towers in Scotland. Such towers were typical of Ireland and may reflect Gaelic patronage for this ancient Pictish monastery.
HISTORIC SCOTLAND/CROWN COPYRIGHT

an altar base. It was designed to grace some, now lost, architectural setting. The framing elements display an assured command of Celtic sculptural idiom, while the central panel shows a familiarity with Classical sculptural conventions found in Late Antique Continental carving. The main panel brings together a complex array of images, which have been convincingly interpreted as representing David, the Old Testament shepherd-warrior-king. One conclusion to be drawn from this imagery is that Pictish kings sought to identify themselves with the ancient king of God's chosen people. Presumably they wished to emphasise that the Picts too were a chosen people.

The St Andrews' Sarcophagus
The central panel features images which link King David of the Old Testament, shown rending the jaws of the lion, with Pictish sovereignty. Made about AD 800 as a piece of church furniture, it is unknown whether it served as an altar, reliquary or tomb.
HISTORIC SCOTLAND/CROWN COPYRIGHT

Sculpture from Meigle
Amongst the large collection of sculpture dating to the ninth–eleventh centuries is this richly carved cross-slab. The reverse side shows (from the top down) a group of mounted warriors with hounds and an angel, above Daniel in the lions' den and at the bottom are various mythological figures including a centaur.
RCHAMS

The pre-eminence of St Andrews is marked out by the large surviving collection of early medieval sculpture, second only to Iona in quantity. Impressive collections of sculpture are essentially all that remains of two other Pictish monasteries at Meigle, Perthshire, and St Vigean's, Angus. The sculpture provides our only insight into the refined artistic and intellectual environment of these historically invisible communities. Their invisibility is probably a consequence of the growth in importance of the cult of Columba and with it the Gaelic church during the ninth and tenth centuries. Sculpture is not the best indication of an early church, but given the patchy historical record, it is often our only evidence. For instance, apart from the mention in the account of Constantine II's proclamation at Scone, it would be easy to overlook the early church at Scone because there is only a single fragment from New Scone.

Cross-slab Fragment from New Scone
This is the only physical evidence for an early church at Scone.
RCAHMS

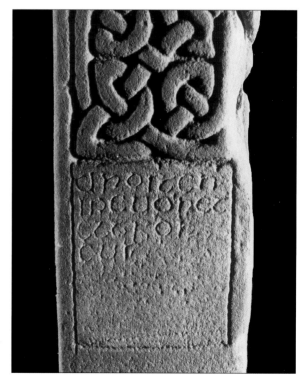

Cross-slab from St Vigean's, Angus
This cross in high relief is one from the large collection of sculpture at what must have been a major Pictish church.
HISTORIC SCOTLAND/CROWN COPYRIGHT

Inscription on the Cross-slab from St Vigean's
This inscription indicates that it was dedicated to Saint Drostan under the patronage of the Pictish king Uoret (839-42).
HISTORIC SCOTLAND/CROWN COPYRIGHT

The new Gaelic Church

The cult of Columba made its first important step in the east when Iona founded the monastery of Lindisfarne in 633 at the invitation of the Northumbrian king Oswald. Under this Gaelic leadership, Lindisfarne quickly grew into a great monastery in its own right, but it maintained a close connection to its mother house. The regular traffic between the monasteries was made easier by a network of churches situated along the main routes through the west Highlands and south through Lothian. Dunkeld was probably amongst the religious houses which served as staging posts for the Columban family. Some of these, like Inchcolm and Inchmahome, were revived as monastic communities during the later Middle Ages, but others simply became parish churches, as at Cramond. This was the most extensive organisation of religious houses in

Major Church Sites *c.* AD 900–1000

The leading churches as indicated by historical sources or the presence of sculpture.

LORRAINE MACEWAN

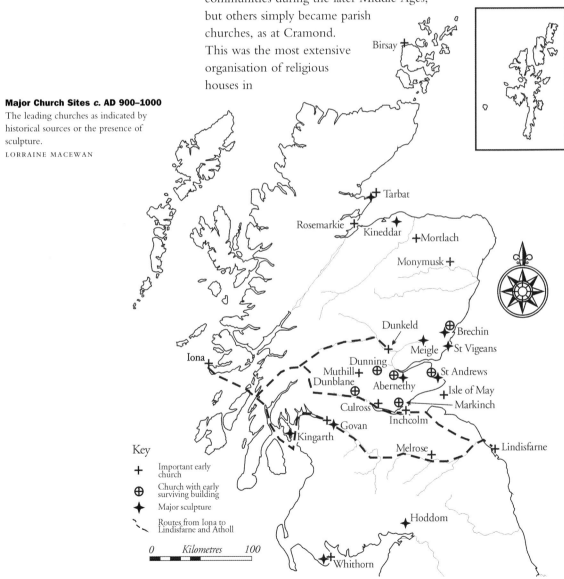

Birsay

Tarbat

Rosemarkie Kineddar Mortlach

Monymusk

Dunkeld Brechin

Meigle St Vigeans

Iona

Dunning

Muthill St Andrews

Dunblane Abernethy

Culross Isle of May

Markinch

Govan Inchcolm

Kingarth

Melrose Lindisfarne

Key

+ Important early church

⊕ Church with early surviving building

✦ Major sculpture

Routes from Iona to Lindisfarne and Atholl

Hoddom

0   Kilometres   100

Whithorn

northern Britain and provided the infrastructure when the centre of the cult of Columba was transferred from Iona to the east.

By the time that Cinaed mac Ailpín had Columba's relics moved to Dunkeld in 848/9, the saint was long established as the patron of the Gaelic royal kindred, Cenél nGabráin. His relics were recognised widely as a source of powerful battle magic that conferred military success to the Gaels. In short, by the ninth century Columba had not only become the chief Gaelic saint, he had become an indispensable talismsan of Gaelic success. The choice of Dunkeld as the new home is slightly puzzling. Although it is in Atholl, with its long-established Gaelic community, the name Dunkeld, 'fort of the Caledonians', suggests a previous importance, perhaps as a tribal centre analogous to Dumbarton or Moncrieff Hill. The fort on King's Seat, Dunkeld, 1.5 kilometres upstream from the church, towers over the Tay as it tumbles out of the Highlands and, although unexcavated, seems the obvious candidate for an ancient tribal centre.

King's Seat, Dunkeld
Upstream from the church and modern village in the middle distance stands the prominent knoll overlooking the Tay crowned by the hillfort which gave the place its name, 'fort of the Caledonians'.
HISTORIC SCOTLAND/CROWN COPYRIGHT

The few fragments of sculpture housed within the ruined Gothic cathedral scarcely hint at Dunkeld's former glory. The chief surviving relic of Columba is similarly understated. The small church-shaped container, now known as the Monymusk Reliquary after its late medieval keeping place, could scarcely hold more than a few finger bones. Apparently that was enough. The shrine was provided with straps so that it could be easily carried in procession and into battle. It is now in the National Museum of Scotland.

The real importance of Dunkeld is revealed by the lineage and activities of its abbots, who were descended from the Cenél nGabrain. They were among the leading Gaelic nobles, and, like their Irish counterparts, were known to lead men into battle. The most famous of these abbots, Crinan (about 1020–45), was the father of Duncan I and led a revolt against Macbeth in 1045. The notion of an abbot as warlord was not a contradiction at the time, particularly in view of Columba's martial powers. There is a suggestion that Dunkeld supported an intellectual community as well. The little we know of late ninth-century political events may well come from a set of annals (a primitive form of chronicle) which was kept at Dunkeld.

Unrelated to the political forces encouraging the growth of the influence of Columba and the rise of Dunkeld was a religious reform movement which swept through Ireland and throughout the

Images of Religious Figures
These clerics on one of the Meigle cross-slabs are shown wearing the distinctive high-necked cowl of monks.

Gaelic-speaking world of the Viking Age. The Céli Dé or Culdee ('servants of god') communities sought to reform a society whose moral failings were widely believed to have been punished by the arrival of the Vikings. The religious customs which Constantine II sought to introduce in 906 may in part have been inspired by this movement. Certainly, a great many of the ancient monastic houses became associated with the Céli Dé: Abernethy, St Andrews and Culross to name just three.

Cathedrals and parishes

The idea of ecclesiastical territories ruled over by a bishop, took hold early in those developed parts of the Roman Empire which had cities and existing regional systems of government. In areas beyond the Empire, like Scotland and Ireland, there was no ready-made administrative structure and as a result the ecclesiastical administration was longer in taking shape. The four oldest documented bishop's seats are all found in what was Pictland and probably assumed their importance during this period of Gaelic rule. The formal designation of episcopal territories dates from the reign of David I in the early 1100s. St Andrews, as we have seen, was a Pictish royal foundation, but it was not until the eleventh century that it emerged as the leading ecclesiastic centre in the kingdom. Before then, Columba's Dunkeld was the main church, while the other early bishoprics, Dunblane and Brechin, were of only regional importance.

The Monymusk Reliquary
This small church-shaped shrine once held bones of St Columba which brought the Scots victory in battle. Part of the arrangement for a strap to carry the reliquary can still be seen.

The path to regional superiority was not always clear-cut. Dunblane only obtained episcopal status after seeing off its local rival in Muthill. At Dunblane there is some Pictish sculpture which hints at its early importance, but the original home of its patron, Blane, was at Kingarth on the island of Bute. His relics were shifted east at about the same time as those of Columba were moved to Dunkeld. The impressive free-standing towers (square at Dunblane and round at Brechin) mark them out as the leading churches in the Pictish regions of Fortriu and Angus prior to their elevation.

There were probably bishops elsewhere but we have no records for them. Whithorn almost certainly had a bishop by the tenth century,

Dunblane Cross-slab
This sculpture exhibits many Pictish characteristics but its unusual design may suggest a Gaelic influence.
KATHERINE FORSYTH

St Serf's Church, Dunning
Built around 1100, this is one of the earliest surviving parish churches in Scotland. Its square tower is reminiscent of those at St Andrews and Dunblane and was surely intended to emphasise the status of the thane of Dunning. The Dupplin Cross is now housed here.
HISTORIC SCOTLAND/CROWN COPYRIGHT

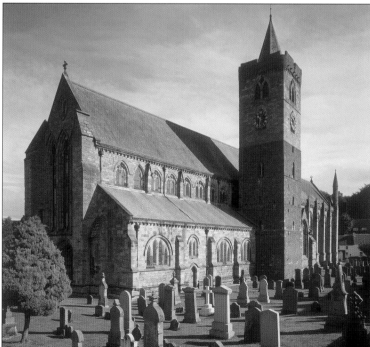

Dunblane Tower
The square tower when built around 1100 was a free standing bell-tower analogous to the round towers of Abernethy and Brechin. It became such an important feature, perhaps because it housed relics, that the Gothic cathedral of the thirteenth century was wrapped around it.
HISTORIC SCOTLAND/CROWN COPYRIGHT

THE CHURCH MATURES 47

Procession of Relics of St Columba at Dunkeld

This reconstruction shows how the reliquary may have been displayed as part of a ceremonial progress around the precinct.
CHRIS BROWN

when an extraordinary set of sculptures began to be erected in the parishes which form the core of its diocese. These crosses have distinctive round heads on interlaced shafts. They are so similar as to suggest that they were carved at, or with the approval of, the great religious centre of Whithorn, perhaps as a sign of association with it.

Given the extraordinary longevity and importance of the church, there were probably bishops at Govan during the tenth and eleventh centuries. Understandably, the later Bishops of Glasgow (from 1114–18) were not keen to draw attention to episcopal rivals. Similarly, we may speculate that there was a bishop in Moray, perhaps in the area of Elgin, because of the presence of sculpture at Kineddar, but there is no contemporary historical evidence (see illustration on page 17). To the north and west of Mortlach (Dufftown), there were no bishops apart from those in the diocese of Sodor based on the Isle of Man and under Norwegian control. In Lothian and the south-east, the Bishop of Durham exercised a firm superiority which allowed no rivals to develop. Elsewhere, for example at Old Aberdeen, the dedication and surviving sculptural fragments at St Machar's indicate the presence of an important church, and we may wonder whether it had a bishop before the twelfth century.

A bishop requires a major church, but that alone is not sufficient. The basic building blocks of a diocese are its parishes. When the historical record begins to become fuller in the twelfth century, parishes are plentiful and well-formed. In many cases, the communities represented by parishes corresponded to areas of secular lordship. The earliest of these secular units in eastern Scotland, north and south of the Forth, were known as *thanages*, because their immediate lords were *thanes* (see page 57). In such circumstances the parish territory may simply indicate the area occupied by the community served by an existing church.

Romanesque architecture

The most impressive expressions of religious devotion to survive from the ninth to eleventh centuries were monumental stone sculptures. There were very few stone-built churches at this time; indeed, buildings were predominantly timber-built. The stone church that existed at Forteviot, represented by the sculpted arch, was exceptional. However, it appears that in the eleventh century building in stone became more common, at least for churches. This beginning of masonry architecture spelled the end for monumental sculpture; patrons began to contribute to the much more costly effort of building churches. For patrons, churches had several advantages over sculpture; not only were they much more visible, but they provided a setting for the most important events of the dynastic life cycle: baptism, marriage, and death. Above all, they show that Christian worship had assumed a more central place in the social life of the community and in the ceremonial activities of the élite.

While the organisation of the Church into dioceses was one measure of increasing episcopal orthodoxy in Scotland, a more visible indication is seen in the quality of the churches themselves. With the exception of a chapel on Iona, all the oldest surviving masonry churches are found in the East Midlands. The earliest of these are free-standing towers or feature towers. This interest in height is one of the most striking aspects of this new architecture. Masonry towers allowed the devotion of the builders to be evident to all and for bells of the holy offices to be heard more widely. In addition to free-standing towers (round at Abernethy and Brechin or square at Dunblane and Muthill), the towers were integrated into the main church structure in more ambitious buildings, as at St Rule's in St Andrews, Markinch in Fife and Dunning in Perthshire.

Although in most cases the buildings are decorated simply and reveal only the lightest of Romanesque influences, there can be little question that this was an élite architecture. The earliest examples are found at the leading churches. Although Abernethy's tower post-dates its high point of prestige, the abbey

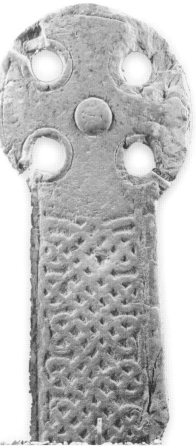

Whithorn Cross
The wheel-headed cross from Whithorn is one of a series of similar crosses that were erected in the neighbouring parishes to display their association with the cathedral.
HISTORIC SCOTLAND/CROWN COPYRIGHT

remained one of the best endowed religious communities in the country. Most of the new churches boasted royal connections, while the others, Markinch and Dunning, were found in thanages. Without question the finest of these early Romanesque churches is St Rule's at the heart of the monastic precinct of St Andrews, whose square tower is 33 metres high and has been built to an exceptionally fine standard. Even allowing for the missing portions, it was a small church, which would have been dwarfed by the great cathedral erected during the twelfth century. Nevertheless, when it was built (starting around 1100), it must have been the most impressive church in the kingdom.

St Rule's Church, St Andrews
The soaring tower of this church from the later eleventh century was probably one of several small churches within the precinct of St Andrews, but it is the only one to have survived.

The Book of Deer

Illumination of the evangelist St Matthew surrounded by Gaelic notes made in the early twelfth century describing the grants of property made to the abbey.

The Book of Deer

Nothing remains of the monastery at Old Deer, some 16 kilometres upriver from Peterhead, but it appears to have been one of the leading churches in Buchan, which claimed to have been founded by Columba himself. The name Deer comes from doire, Gaelic for oak, an etymology it shares with other Columban monasteries like Derry and Durrow (in Ireland). It contains an invaluable set of notes on the property of the monastery of Old Deer, beginning with an account of its foundation by Columba himself.

The Book of Deer is the only illuminated manuscript to survive from early medieval Scotland. In contrast to the most famous of the insular manuscripts (e.g. the Books of Kells and Lindisfarne, this 'splendid little book' was not intended for display, but was intended to be used. This small, handy volume (15.4 x 10.7 cm) is modestly illuminated and was probably made at Deer itself around 900. The book contains the gospels and certain liturgies for the sick and dying. Over the subsequent centuries the book itself became an object of veneration, and was possibly even regarded as a relic with healing properties.

When Moray and Buchan were finally subdued by the Scots in the early 1100s, the monks began to compile records of their landholding, either because they were trying to regain lost territories or to protect them. They used their most valuable book – the Book of Deer – to record their properties. The notes were written in Gaelic and are unique as records of the system of lordship that prevailed in pre-Norman times.

The notes record various grants made by a number of nobles over a period of about 100 years or so. These grants reveal two grades of nobility below the king: mormaer and tioseach. The tioseach was the head of a kindred, who exercised lordship over a district. The mormaer was also the head of a kindred, but in addition he enjoyed superiority over various kindreds. These regional magnates owed loyalty to the king and were responsible for leading the men of their region as required. In effect the mormaer was the lord of a large, discrete region, later to be known as an earldom, which he held independently of the king. These earldoms may have originated as independent Pictish kingdoms.

The notes reveal that all of these lords were entitled to tribute from the land they held, which must have been rendered in kind, as livestock or other produce, and the tribute could be granted to a beneficiary. Not only did the lords make grants of the tribute, but they also made outright grants of the land to the monks.

These notes have tremendous implications for our understanding of landholding and lordship during the Gaelic kingdom. What they make clear is that there were well-established mechanisms for the management of land, for a sort of taxation, and that there was a level of personal of ownership over land, which allowed it to be handed over permanently to the Church. The book itself reminds us that the Dark Ages were not quite as dark as is sometimes thought. Indeed, had Scotland's subsequent religious history been less traumatic, more evidence of learning, scholarship and administration would survive.

Lordship over the Land

Agriculture and political economy

Status and wealth in early medieval Scotland were measured largely in terms of the resources of the country. The number of cattle one possessed and the number of men at arms one could call upon were the most critical measures. In the absence of coinage, cattle served as a kind of currency, while the number of fighting men one commanded was the ultimate indication of lordly power. From an early time, possibly in the fifth century, a system of lordship developed over much of Britain from Wales and the English Midlands northwards, under which the lord (usually a king of some description) would move between a number of centres within his realm. While in residence at these centres, the lord would exercise his authority by holding court, resolving local disputes, and dispensing hospitality to an extended group that included his household, officials, followers and members of the local community. Revenue from the district around the centre was collected here and, when the lord was in residence, consumed by the royal entourage.

The Forth Valley and the Ochils
At harvest time the richness of the East Midlands is plain.
STEPHEN T. DRISCOLL

In Scotland the areas around these centres were known as *shires* and included a number of outlying settlements and villages. They were the precursors of parishes and in some cases correspond exactly with the ecclesiastical divisions. The shires were administered for the king by royal officials who collected the revenues, organised the services to be performed and oversaw the use of common resources such as grazing lands, the mill and peat banks. These officials were known as *thanes* and as a result the shire centres were known as *thanages*. These terms are of Anglo-Saxon derivation and suggest that they were coined during those periods when Scotland enjoyed superiority over the Lothians and Northumbria. The process of formalising the shire system may have started early in the tenth century under Constantine II (900–43); it would have continued under his son Indulf (954–62), who conquered Edinburgh, and was probably consolidated during the reign of Malcolm II (1005–34), whose victory at Carham in 1018 secured the River Tweed as the border.

Hunting Scene from the Drostan Stone, St Vigean's
This unique depiction of a hunter using a cross-bow departs from the conventional image of mounted hunters.
HISTORIC SCOTLAND/CROWN COPYRIGHT

This system of shires and thanes provided the means of using what was essentially an Iron Age economy to sustain a noble class and to fuel royal power. In most respects it is difficult to distinguish early medieval farming activities from those of the Iron Age. The main cereal crops (barley and oats, rarely wheat or rye) were the same, the livestock (cattle, sheep and pigs) were the same, even the farms on the better land were in more or less the same place that they had been for centuries. Cattle were most important: the largest proportion of the meat consumed was beef, but milk and cheese were probably even of greater nutritional significance. In the Highlands and the less fertile areas, wild foods contributed more to the diet, but generally few wild animals were consumed. Indeed, archaeologists usually interpret wild animal remains as evidence of recreational hunting by the aristocracy.

Settlements and social status

Almost everyone had a direct involvement with agricultural production, as land owner, free farmer or unfree peasant. A modest amount is known about the chief settlements, ie the thanages and monasteries, which controlled extensive lands and numerous subordinate settlements. Judging from twelfth-century evidence about social organisation, the free-born were a significant element of the population, but probably not a majority. Amongst the unfree peoples there were degrees of dependence ranging from the tenant, to the *neyf* bound to the land like a serf. There was even some slavery. Free-born subjects were obliged to render to their lord a mixture of agricultural produce, such as cattle and cereal, and to perform some honourable services, which included military duty; unfree subjects also rendered agricultural products, frequently of a less prestigious nature, and were obliged to provide labour services, which included menial tasks like road maintenance.

Although the labour of dependant peoples accounted for the bulk of the food production, little is known of their lives, as they were not written about or portrayed in sculpture. It is only through archaeological investigations of lower status settlements such as those

Buckquoy Sequence

The Pictish period occupation was largely obliterated by the Norse settlers who seized the farm in the ninth century.

LORRAINE MACEWAN

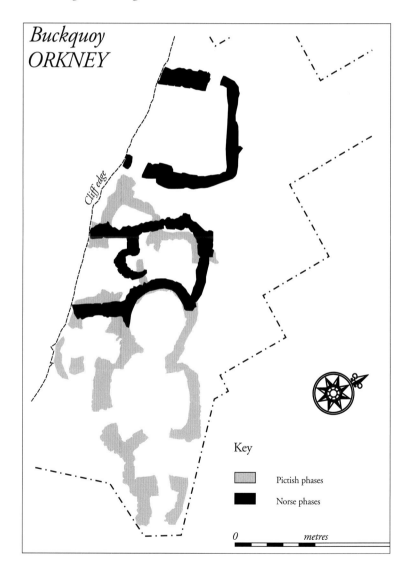

Buckquoy
ORKNEY

Cliff edge

Key

Pictish phases

Norse phases

0   *metres*

at Buckquoy, Orkney, or Easter Kinnear, Fife, that we gain insight into the lives of the majority of people in early medieval Scotland.

Buckquoy is situated on the mainland opposite the tidal island of the Brough of Birsay, on some of the richest land in the Northern Isles. This remarkable farmstead straddles the period of the Pictish-Norse transition and this shows in its architectural remains. Barley and oats were the main crops and cattle the main livestock, as indeed they remain to this day in that area. Despite the milder climate and richer soil, a similar farming regime was followed to that at Easter Kinnear some 250 kilometres to the south. What was conspicuously different was the architecture of the houses. In Orkney, where the stone is so easily worked, this was the preferred building material. With the arrival of the Norse, the Pictish house at Buckquoy was replaced during the 800s by a typical Norse bow-walled longhouse. This striking change did little to alter the size or comfort of the building, but clearly reflected a change in architectural taste associated with Norse political domination.

At Easter Kinnear, suitable building stone was not readily available, so the buildings were constructed using oaks posts and wattle and daub walls. These ancient building materials were used throughout Lowland Scotland, but at Easter Kinnear we have the earliest evidence of them being used in a new way. Here the Iron Age tradition of round house architecture was abandoned in favour of a rectangular design. Buildings were made roughly square with load-bearing walls and the earliest examples had shallow cellars. Since this part of Fife is prime cereal-growing country, these cellars were presumably for grain storage. The rectangular design had no local precedent and must have been inspired by developments in élite architecture, particularly the great timber halls which began to be built at Northumbrian royal centres in the seventh century, as for instance at Dunbar, from whence they spread north.

Thanages and Political Regions of Scotia

This map shows the main political division within Scotia around AD 1000, when the system of thanages probably began to take shape.
LORRAINE MACEWAN

Buckquoy has been regarded as the dwelling of a freeman, but
given its position it seems more likely to have been a dependant
settlement of the Brough of Birsay. It was probably one of a series of
farms strung out along the Bay of Birsay, forming a sort of extended
township.

At Easter Kinnear the excavated buildings were
tightly clustered into small hamlets of three or
four dwellings, which were clearly subordinate
settlements of the estate centred at the
modern farm where the ruins of the
medieval castle are located. The material
culture of the people who worked the
land was extremely poor; only stone
artefacts (querns, whetstones and a lamp)
were recovered. Despite this apparent
poverty, however, these were
'successful' settlements that were
frequently rebuilt, and which were
occupied from the sixth until the
thirteenth century, if not later. The
Kinnear estate prospered and eventually
the squarish peasant dwellings were
replaced by the narrow, rectangular
longhouse which typified late medieval
rural settlement.

Landscape management and regional power

Long-term political power thus relied upon the effective
control of the land. At the grassroots level we see at Easter Kinnear
the means by which large farms were organised to produce a surplus

that could sustain the lowest level of gentry. In social terms, these farms, estates and shires could be organised along kinship lines, with extended families controlling the key positions and working together. This is probably how the early post-Roman kingdoms were run, but there are practical limits to how big an area can be effectively ruled by family and kin.

The Gaelic kings seem to have been able to transcend these limitations by making good use of the shires, which not only provided an effective means of taxation, but also, through the thane, allowed the kings greater control of the more remote parts of the kingdom. To some extent the thanages served as a mechanism for overcoming distance, since the king routinely would visit all corners of the kingdom and his subjects could have regular contact. Nevertheless, given the geographic and cultural make-up of Scotland, the accomplishment of the Gaelic kings of Alba who constructed a kingdom that stretched from Inverness to Carlisle must rank with the great accomplishments of early medieval state-building.

The Settlement of Easter Kinnear
A reconstruction of the settlement as it might have appeared around AD 900.
CHRIS BROWN

Mounted Warrior from the Govan Sarcophagus
Like the Pictish representations, the central figure in this British sculpture is prepared to lead men into battle or to pursue the hunt.

TOM GRAY

Expanding the Gaelic Kingdom

At the start of the ninth century the rise in Gaelic political prospects could not have been predicted. For most of the preceding century the kings of Dál Riata were subordinate to the Pictish kings. What is more, the Pictish heartlands seem to have escaped the initial Viking onslaught, while the Hebrides felt the full force of the raiders. Iona, for instance, suffered six attacks before 824. All of this changed in a single disastrous battle fought in 839 by the 'gentiles' (i.e. Vikings) against the 'men of Fortiu' who fell 'almost without number'. Among the slain were the Pictish king with his brother and their ally the King of Dál Riata. Because there was no natural successor, a civil war ensued, lasting from 842 until 849, during the course of which Cinaed mac Ailpín (843–58) emerged as the most powerful warlord. Traditionally, he is said to have secured the Pictish kingship by treacherously killing his rival at Scone, but the truth is that we do not know the manner of his triumph. There are few contemporary sources and we do not even know where he came from. In the tenth century the kinglists of Dál Riata were doctored to provide him with a royal pedigree and to suggest that previous kings had also ruled over both the Scots and the Picts. Cinaed must have been a superior military leader, but we can only speculate as to the personal qualities or connections that allowed him to unite Picts and Scots against the Vikings.

Not only was Cinaed's realm secure from the Vikings, but he aggressively sought to utilise his military strength to exploit weakness in Northumbria. The six raids he led against the English were a major factor in the collapse of the Northumbrian kingdom and laid the groundwork for the conquest of the Lothians. Cinaed's place in history was secured in part by these military exploits, but ultimately comes from the success of his descendants in establishing a long-lasting dynasty, which was to rule for most of the next two centuries.

The Vikings did return in the 860s and 870s and Cinaed's sons and grandsons spent a great deal of energy dealing with repeated challenges. The mac Ailpín dynasty weathered a major defeat at Dollar, Clackmannanshire, in 875, the temporary loss of the throne in the 880s and a defeat at Dunottar, in the Mearns, in 893, when the king was killed. The final round in the bout with the Vikings was fought by Constantine II, grandson of Cinaed and one of Scotland's most outstanding kings. Not only did he see off the Vikings once and for all, but he established a kingdom in Scotland that was sturdy enough to withstand the pressures of increasingly ambitious English monarchs.

The Viking problem occupied much of Constantine II's first six years, but by 906 he was secure enough to begin a programme of national reconstruction, which began with his commitment to uphold the laws of the Church made at Scone. This was a crucial moment in shaping Gaelic national identity, and from about this time the kingdom of the Picts is referred to as Alba. By 918 Constantine II was sufficiently powerful that the Earl of Northumbria, who by now no longer used the title king, sought the help of the Scots against the York Vikings. Constantine was effective enough for the Northumbrians to choose to remain under his protection and this introduced Gaelic interest into the Lothians. Within Britain, Constantine's only rival was Athelstan, the ambitious King of Wessex, who in 934 invaded deep into Scotland and forced Constantine to take refuge at Dunottar. Constantine survived to fight another day and in 937 he led a great alliance of Scots, northern British and Dublin Vikings into battle against the English at Brunanburh, a battle every bit as pivotal as Bannockburn.

Mounted Warrior from the Dupplin Cross
This image probably represents a Pictish king in his most crucial role, as war leader.
HISTORIC SCOTLAND/CROWN COPYRIGHT

Warrior from Meigle
This small gravestone portrays the equipment of a mounted warrior in some detail.
HISTORIC SCOTLAND/CROWN COPYRIGHT

Brunanburh – the great battle

Constantine led the invasion force deep into Northumbria in the autumn of 937, before meeting Athelstan in a great battle, which may have been fought in the Don Valley, Yorkshire. A poetic passage in the *Anglo-Saxon Chronicle* celebrates the valour of their warrior king and the victory seemingly bestowed by God:

'At this time king Athelstan, lord over earls and his warriors' ring-giver, and his brother too, the prince Edmund, won by the edges of their swords life-long glory in battle about Brunanburh.

They sliced through the shield-wall and hacked the linden battle-targes with swords, the legacies of hammers, these sons of Edward, since it was inborn in them from their forbears that they should often, in warfare against every foe, defend land, treasure-hoard and homes. The aggressors yielded; Scots and Vikings fell dying. The field grew wet with men's blood from when in the morning-tide that glorious star, the sun, glided aloft and over the earth's plains, the bright candle of God the everlasting Lord, to when the noble creation sank to rest.'

In *Egil's Saga* the setting and passage of the battle are described in detail from the perspective of Egil, the Viking hero-poet serving in Athelstan's army. The battle was hard-fought and desperate, but eventually the Scots were forced to retreat and 'everyone caught running away was put to death'. Egil celebrates his contribution to this grim work in a poem that concludes with the traditional image of slaughter, a glutted raven.

West over water
I wallowed in the slain-stack,
Angry, my Adder [Egil's sword] struck
Adils [a Welsh king] in the battle-storm.
Olaf [king of Dublin] played the steel-game,
The English his enemies;
Hring [a Welsh king] sought the raging blades,
No ravens went hungry.

There were great losses on both sides and although Constantine and his allies were forced to withdraw, the collective display of strength dented Athelstan's ambition to rule all of Britain and helped to secure Scotland's future independence.

After 43 years of rule, having secured the long-term future of the Gaelic kingdom, Constantine II retired to become a monk at St Andrews. At his retirement the area ruled by the king of Scots (as he may now be called) ran from the Mounth to the Forth and he was overlord of Northumbria. The neighbouring kingdoms of Cumbria (including Strathclyde) and Moray may have also acknowledged his

Penrith Hogbacks
A setting of four hogback gravestones at St Andrew's Church. The position may not be original.
STEPHEN T DRISCOLL

overlordship. Beyond that a string of independent polities stretched around the northern and western perimeter of the kingdom, including the earldom of Orkney (with Caithness), a fledgling kingdom of the Isles, and the kingdom of Galloway.

The reign of Constantine II was exceptionally long by medieval standards and provided a stable political basis for the Gaelic kingdom. This stability is apparent in the royal succession over the next two centuries which included a number of other long reigns: Malcolm II (1005–34), Macbeth (1040–57), Malcolm III (1058–93) and David I (1124–53). During this period Cumbria and Moray were annexed and the border with England established.

Acquisition of Cumbria and Moray

Only the final stages of the annexation of Cumbria are known with any certainty; prior to that we are largely dependent on archaeological evidence. The northern Britons were on the front line during the Viking Age, because the Clyde proved an attractive alternative to the overland route between Dublin and the east coast of Northumbria and a convenient refuge from the main theatres of war in northern England and the Irish Sea. The pivotal moment in the history of the Clyde was the sack of Dumbarton in 870. However, the kingdom was not without power and influence.

King Owen of Cumbria was a prominent figure in the conflict with Wessex and was an ally of Constantine II at the Battle of Brunanburh (937), where he was slain. Although this suggests that Constantine II enjoyed a degree of overkingship in Cumbria, it was not until the native dynasty died out in 1020s that Malcolm II made his grandson, Duncan, ruler of Cumbria. Prior to that, Cumbria appears to have enjoyed a degree of independence and to have enjoyed military success, extending its rule as far south as Penrith.

Apart from their sculpture we have no contemporary expressions of these northern British peoples. The repertoire is mostly limited to cross-slabs and few are executed at the same scale seen at Govan.

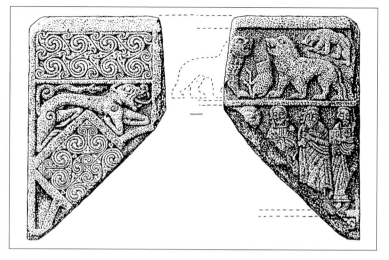

Tarbat Cross-slab

This is a small fragment of what was once a massive cross-slab was found reused in the fabric of the church at Portmahomack, Easter Ross. Evidence from the York University excavations suggests that the cross was smashed in a Viking raid.

M CARVER

The Barochan Cross

Perhaps the finest of the British crosses from Strathclyde. Previously it stood on the Renfrewshire escarpment overlooking the Clyde, but it is now housed in Paisley Abbey.

STEPHEN T. DRISCOLL

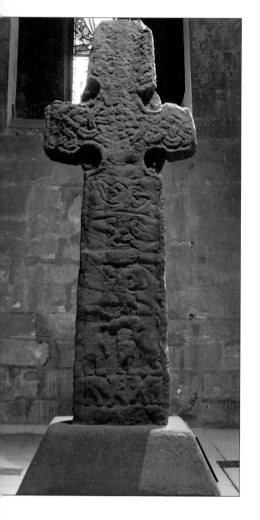

However, there are a few impressive pieces such as the Barochan Cross, Renfrewshire. Outside Govan the Norse influence is not prominent in the sculpture. The distribution of this sculpture at key political centres suggests that the parish system was taking shape in Strathclyde in the tenth and eleventh centuries, as it was in Alba.

Moray was also on the front-line, facing the ambitious Orkney earls. The ruling dynasty here traced their ancestry through the Cenél Loairn, a junior kindred within Dál Riata. They presumably migrated into northern Pictland at about the same time as their cousin Cinaed and his followers moved into Fortriu. Prior to the late 900s there is no evidence that the kings of Fortriu, or their Alban successors, exercised any sovereignty north of the Mounth. Nevertheless, during the tenth century, agreement was reached whereby the dynasty of Fortriu and that of Moray would alternate holding the kingship of Scone. Although this seems awkward, similar arrangements existed in contemporary Ireland, most notably for the kingship of Tara. Naturally such agreements cause problems when one side refuses to play the game, as happened in the case of Macbeth. Evidently Duncan, son of Malcolm II, usurped the Scone kingship when it was the turn of the men of Moray, so Macbeth took it by force in 1040. After a period of secure rule, his reign was ended in 1057 by Malcolm III, son of Duncan, with the help of the Earl of Northumbria.

Like the northern British, we know little of the men of Moray apart from their sculpture, but this is exquisite. The best of this sculpture is associated with the extensive ecclesiastical estates of Easter Ross, including the recently excavated monastery of Tarbat. This sculpture provides a vivid view of aristocratic life, which suggests that the leaders did little more than hunt, fight and pray. For scale the most impressive sculpture is the Sueno's stone, Forres. One side of this 7-metre-high cross-slab is covered with a battle scene of saga-like complexity. Presumably this represents an epic triumph over the Vikings, but the events depicted are not described anywhere else. It is also important in that it is perhaps the last sculpture to be executed in the tradition initiated by the Picts. Following the death of Macbeth, Moray was subjected to constant military pressure from the south, and by the early twelfth century, when the final Moray succession attempts were quashed, patronage had moved on from sculpture to the church buildings.

The southern border: Lothian and Northumbria

The conquest of the Lothians began with Cinaed mac Ailpín's raids into Northumbria during the ninth century, which contributed to destabilising the kingdom. By the tenth century, Northumbrians were looking to their powerful northern neighbours for support against the Vikings and later against Wessex. Edinburgh came under the control of the Scots during the reign of Indulf (954–62) presumably along with much of Lothian. It was not until the Battle of Carham in 1018, when Malcolm II triumphed over the Earl of Bamburgh, that the border was fixed at the Tweed. This did not end Scottish involvement in Northumbria, which provided refuge to the juvenile Malcolm III and then supported him against Macbeth. Intrigues continued into the eleventh century, culminating in 1066 with the failed attempt to seize the English throne by a combined force of Norse, Orcadian and Northumbrian chancers. Malcolm III had hoped to profit from the invasion, but in the event William the Conqueror was the main beneficiary. Malcolm presumably felt that years of overlordship entitled Scotland to the land as far south as the Tyne. His support for the disenfranchised Northumbrian earls and his reckless raids into northern England in 1070 were an annoyance to William the Conqueror. So in 1072 William brought a great army into Scotland and at Abernethy he forced Malcolm to do homage. For the remainder of the century the Scotland was technically subject to the Norman kings, but this had little impact, as the Normans were never interested in acquiring the north. Indeed, they placed their northern frontier castles in the unthreatening positions of Newcastle-upon-Tyne (1080) and Carlisle (1092).

The periphery: Galloway, Orkney and the Isles

As the Viking wars died out at the end of the tenth century, small principalities developed in the gaps between the two great powers of England and Scotland. All of the small polities could claim an ancient regional identity, but traced their political ancestry to the Norse. In the shadow of the Isle of Man, Galloway appeared first as a

Sueno's Stone, Forres
The largest of all Scottish cross-slabs stands outside Forres. On the side opposite the cross is an extremely complex set of images which is a war epic in stone. This may have been amongst the last of the cross-slabs to be erected.
HISTORIC SCOTLAND/CROWN COPYRIGHT

dependency of the Manx kings and later as an independent kingdom. The importance of the Norse settlers in the south-west is evident in the name adopted for the place. *Gall-Gháidhil*, 'foreign Gael', is an Irish term used to describe mixed Norse and Gaelic Vikings and is the source of the word Galloway.

At Whithorn, although the Anglian monastery was destroyed, presumably by some unrecorded Viking raid, it did not disappear. Indeed, it remade itself into a trading centre in the Norse manner and the church persisted. During the course of the tenth and eleventh centuries Whithorn took steps towards episcopal status by establishing a network of parishes, which are marked out by the uniformity of their sculptured crosses (see page 49).

One of the few secular strongholds of this period to have been excavated is Cruggleton, which occupies a headland on the Whithorn peninsula. Here a rampart of timber and earth enclosed a compound containing a rectangular timber hall and various outbuildings. This description of Somerled's castle in Galloway might equally apply to it:

> Upon a great dark-coloured rock
> He had his house right nobly set,
> Built all about with wattle-work.
> Upon the summit was a tower
> That was not made of stone and lime
> Of earth the wall was builded, high,
> And crenellated, battlemented.

Until the mid-twelfth century the lords of Galloway continued to call themselves kings, but due to the smaller size of their kingdom it was only a matter of time before they were brought into the dominion of the Scots. A return to the construction of fortified lordly residences, such as Cruggleton Castle, began an architectural tradition which lasted throughout the rest of the Middle Ages. Castle building was embraced first in those maritime regions where naval power made places vulnerable to rapid attack. Therefore, considering their naval

William the Conqueror at Abernethy
Malcolm III was forced to meet William at the ancient monastery and pay homage after his efforts to assert his claims for overlordship in Northumbria collapsed.
CHRIS BROWN

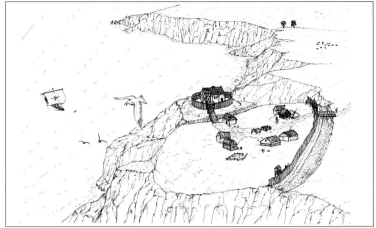

Map of Scotia
By the middle of the eleventh century Scotia was the dominant Kingdom in Northern Britain.

Key
+ Church
● Secular Center
★ Battle

0   Kilometres   100

traditions, it is not surprising that the earliest known castles survive in Orkney and the Hebrides.

In the northern isles, the earldom in Orkney was valued too much by the kings of Norway to allow it independence. With the aid of the Norse Crown and Dublin Vikings, the earls of Orkney extended their dominion south to the Dornoch Firth. The name Dingwall, the meeting place of the 'thing' or Norse assembly, is testimony to the security of their tenure of the north. By the end of tenth century Orkney was a major political force and its rulers were linked by marriage to the courts of Norway, Scotland, and Dublin. Without question the most important person to emerge from this royal environment was Earl Thorfinn the Mighty, who probably matured under the protection of his grandfather Malcolm II.

Thorfinn ruled Orkney for half a century (about 1014–65) and is remembered in saga literature as the greatest earl. He was a fierce war leader who systematically destroyed his rivals within Orkney and sought to extend his rule to the south,

Finlaggan, Islay

The Great Island, site of hall, church and settlement and the smaller Council Island to the rear can be seen to the right of the standing stone. Remarkably for a maritime power, the seat of authority was located in this secluded loch.

KATHERINE FORSYTH

where he fought against the Scottish king, possibly Macbeth. In his later years he embraced Christianity with enthusiasm. He went on pilgrimage to Rome in 1050 and established the first bishop in Orkney around this time. The fine church built at the earl's residence on the Brough of Birsay was the bishop's seat and Thorfinn's final resting place. In due course, Birsay became one of the principal sites associated with the cult of St Magnus. The martyred Magnus developed into the principal saint in the northern islands, and provided a religious figure comparable in importance to Columba, Kentigern, Ninian and Cuthbert. The earliest castles in the north, the best preserved of which is a simple masonry tower known as Cubbie Roo's Castle (a corruption of the builder's name, Kolbein Hrega), seem to have been part of a system of coastal defences built in Orkney.

Little is known of the homeland of the Gaels after the demise of Dál Riata in the ninth century. The Western Isles were known as the *Innse Gall*, 'islands of the foreigners' and served as a staging place for Viking raids. The Norse-Gaelic society that flourished there gave birth to a precarious sea lordship, based on control of the waves, which was ruled from the Isle of Man. It is only in the twelfth century that the Hebrides and Argyll finally regained a degree of independence through the military prowess of Somerled, first King of the Isles (1153–64). At the centre of this kingdom was a place of ancient significance: an island in Finlaggan Loch, Islay. This appears to have developed in part as a royal residence, in part as a place of assembly (in later centuries the Council of the Isles would meet there) and the place where kings were proclaimed using ceremonies drawn from the same cultural tradition as those of Scone and Tara.

Macbeth (1040–57)

Macbeth is the best known usurper in the British literary tradition, but by the standards of his day he was a legitimate and successful king, who conducted himself as any other ambitious ruler. His biography is spare and most of the sources reflect the interests of the victorious party or later prejudices. He was the son of the mormaer (petty king, later synonymous with earl) of Moray, who was slain by a dynastic rival. (Incidentally, this murderous cousin was amongst the patrons of the monastery of Deer recorded in the Gaelic notes in the Book of Deer.) Macbeth himself first appears in the historic record alongside King Malcolm II doing homage to King Cnut in 1031, suggesting that he was a member of the Scottish court. Macbeth ruled Moray and belonged to a royal kindred eligible for the Scottish throne. According to well-established practice, the kingship of Scone alternated between different royal kindreds and when Duncan I (1034–40) claimed the throne, this broke with tradition. Duncan unsuccessfully sought to wrest Caithness from Jarl Thorfinn of Orkney and led a campaign against Northumbria that culminated in a disastrous siege of Durham. Such failures of leadership were fatal to a medieval king, and Macbeth took the opportunity to rebel. Duncan was slain by Macbeth near Elgin, when apparently attempting to subdue Moray. Bloody paths to the throne, such as this, were utterly unremarkable at the time. Macbeth's reign is remembered in various later accounts as a time of plenty, but it was also a bloody time. Early in his reign Duncan's sons, including the future king Malcolm III ('Canmore'), were too young to resist Macbeth's rule, but he had powerful enemies in Atholl, Orkney and Northumbria. In 1045 Crinan, Abbot of Dunkeld and father of Duncan I, was killed leading the men of Atholl against Macbeth. Malcolm Canmore, who had taken refuge with his kinsmen in Northumbria, led his first invasion of Scotland in 1046, which was repulsed by Macbeth. At the height of his reign Macbeth was sufficiently secure to make a pilgrimage to Rome in 1050 (at the same time as Earl Thorfinn). He is the only Scottish king to have made the pilgrimage and when in Rome he is said to have 'scattered silver like seed to the poor', perhaps in emulation of the English King Cnut's extravagant displays of generosity in 1031. At home his generosity is indicated by the grants made with his wife, Gruoch, to the Céli Dé community of St Serf's in Loch Leven.

Ultimately, Malcolm III's superior allies won out. The Earl of Northumberland actively supported the claims of Malcolm III with another invading army in 1054. The decisive Battle of the Seven Sleepers was probably fought near Scone and in the later Middle Ages came to identified with the Iron Age hillfort of Dunsinane. Macbeth was defeated and retreated to the north of the Mounth. In 1057, Macbeth was slain by Malcolm at the strategic stronghold of Lumphanan in Mar, 17 years to the day after he had slain Malcolm's father.

Epilogue: the Decline of the Gaelic Kingdom

In one sense the decline of the Gaelic kingdom can be seen as a consequence of its success at harnessing the energies of different cultural groups. During the eleventh century Scotland was regarded as a major political force in Britain. As a result, the kings of Scots were drawn more into the European world of power politics, particularly the English sphere. The most celebrated relationship is that of David I, son of Malcolm III, who was raised in the English court and held extensive estates, the Honour of Huntingdon, from the English king. When David I (1124–53) became king, he used his experience and a network of personal connections to make sweeping changes to the social and political order, modelled on the feudal institutions developed after the Norman conquest. Not only did this involve the introduction of a large number of knights, but it included the endowment of a number of major monasteries, like Kelso and Melrose, and a new cathedral at Glasgow. The consequences of David I's reign are too extensive to consider here, but they mark a watershed in Scottish history.

One of the new men to emerge during David's reign, was Somerled, Lord of Argyll and Kintyre. Somerled created a personal empire amongst the Gaelic-Norse society of the Hebrides, which for a time he ruled as a loyal subject of the King of Scots, leading his followers in the Battle of the Standard (1138). When David I died, Somerled rebelled against both the King of Scots and the King of Man to establish a Kingdom of the Isles. Inevitably, Somerled's disputes with the King of Scots led to war. Presumably, Somerled considered the lower Clyde to be his territory and sought to enforce this view by doing battle against the principal agents of royal authority – the Stewards of Renfrew and the Bishop of Glasgow. In 1164, Somerled was defeated at Inchinnan, just west of Renfrew, by the forces of the men of Glasgow and the power of St Kentigern. The victory was commemorated in a poem by a Glasgwegian cleric, the *Song on the Death of Somerled*:

> 'So the enemy host being driven off, deluded,
> all the kingdom rang with Kentigern's loud praise.
> A cleric hacked off the head of the wretched leader Somerled,
> and placed it into bishop Herbert's outstretched hands.
> He said, 'The Scottish saints are surely to be praised!'
> yet wept as his custom was, to see the head of his enemy.
> And to blessed Kentigern he attributed victory,
> so keep you his memory always, and that fittingly.'

In many respects Somerled's death marked the beginning of the decline of Gaelic influence in mainland Scotland. After the twelfth century the importance of Gaelic language and culture faded and it never again enjoyed such widespread currency in Scotland. And yet the world shaped during these centuries persisted.

The belief in powerful, protective and vengeful saints, as celebrated in the *Song on the Death of Somerled* and as expressed in widespread devotion to the Scottish saints, lasted for the rest of the Middle Ages. The ethnic and political origins of these saint reveal the components which were brought together in the early medieval Gaelic kingdom of Scotland.

Guthrie Bell Shrine

At one time there would have been many more ornately enshrined examples of objects or bones associated with early medieval saints. However, this shrine from Forfarshire is a rare survival.
NATIONAL MUSEUM OF SCOTLAND

How Do I Find Out More?

Many of the most important places remained significant throughout the Middle Ages. As a result, later building often obscures evidence of earlier eras. However, many of the places are so striking physically that simply being there contributes to appreciating the social and political dynamics of the age.

A number of the sites are open to the public by Historic Scotland (HS) or by other agencies (P). Other sites in private ownership may require permission from the land owner to visit. The Ordnance Survey grid references can be used to locate the sites.

NO 190164 Abernethy, Perthshire (HS) – The round tower dominates the market square of this small village. The eleventh-century tower stands within the enclosure of the Pictish royal monastery which was founded around ad 600 and dedicated to St Brigit. It was here that Malcolm III met William the Conqueror in 1072.

HY 239285 Brough of Birsay, Orkney (HS) – This strong tidal island has been occupied from Pictish times, but most of the numerous dwellings and ecclesiastic remains date to the Norse period. The earl ruled from here and around 1100 built a small Romanesque church, which stands at the heart of the large complex of buildings that formed the palace.

NS 400744 Dumbarton Castle, Dunbartonshire (HS) – The early medieval structures on Clyde Rock were swept away by the Viking raid of 870, but the site retains a monumental impressiveness. Housed within the castle, which is largely of post-medieval date, are two fragments of sculpture considered to be of the Govan school.

NO 024426 Dunkeld Cathedral, Perthshire (HS) – The site is dominated by the partially ruined late medieval cathedral. The church contains some fragments of sculpture which date to the time when Columba's relics were housed here. 1.5 km upstream from the cathedral is King's Seat hillfort (in private ownership).

NO 881838 Dunottar Castle, Kincardineshire (P) – This headland is almost entirely surrounded by the sea and is connected by a heavily defended narrow neck of land. Towering cliVs make this one of the most secure royal strongholds in eastern Scotland and a natural destination for kings seeking refuge, as Constantine II did in 934. Extensive ruins of the medieval castle obscure any traces of the tenth and eleventh centuries, but the site itself is spectacular.

NT 252735 Edinburgh Castle (HS) – The earliest surviving buildings date to the time of David I, but the castle now houses the Stone of Destiny alongside the Scottish regalia. Although the late medieval defences and modern building obscure any earlier structures, the topography of the castle makes it easy to appreciate its timeless strategic value.

NS 553658 Govan Old Parish Church, Glasgow (P) – One of the most impressive collections of early medieval sculpture in Scotland is housed within a Wne Gothic revival church in the heart of urban Glasgow. Its ancient oval churchyard is an oasis

in a post-industrial urban landscape. The collection includes a unique sarcophagus and the largest hogback monuments anywhere. The church is open to visitors on a regular basis and access can be arranged through the Pearce Institute (next to the churchyard).

NM 286245 Iona, Argyll (P) – The island is reached from Fionport on Mull, where there is a new visitor centre. Of greatest interest is the superb collection of sculpture, the largest in Scotland. The later medieval monastery (refounded by Somerled) occupies the site established by Columba, but traces of the earthen enclosure, vallum, are still visible.

NJ 576036 Lumphanan, Aberdeenshire (HS) – A large ring-work castle of the twelfth century is the most obvious feature at the site where Macbeth was slain in 1057. This castle commands a strategic route that runs through Mar and connects Deeside to Speyside.

NO 287445 Meigle, Perthshire (HS) – The collection of sculpture housed within the old schoolhouse at Meigle is one of the most diverse in Scotland. A wide range of monument forms are represented and many are extremely Wnely executed. The quality of the collection probably reflects Pictish royal patronage.

NO 136199 Moncrieff Hill, Perthshire (P) – The hillfort can be reached via a forest walk beginning at the south-east edge of the hill. The fort perched above the southern cliffs commands a great view over the lower Earn valley. The large fort includes several phases of construction, the latest of which is a massively-built dry-stone dun. Also contained within the ramparts is a large artificial pool or well.

NO 513166 St Andrews Cathedral and St Rule's Tower, Fife (HS) – Within the cathedral precinct stands St Rule's Tower, one of the most impressive of all Romanesque churches in Scotland. Views from the tower provide a dramatic panorama and a sweeping prospect of the great ruined monastery. Housed within the cathedral museum is an exceptional collection of sculpture including the St Andrews' Sarcophagus.

NO 638429 St Vigean's, Arbroath, Angus (HS) – The collection of sculpture for which St Vigean's is renowned is housed within a cottage at the foot of the church, which crowns a precipitous little hill. As at Meigle, a wide range of monument types are present, but the style of the sculpture displays a number of features which are distinctive to the site.

NO 114266 Scone Palace, Perthshire (P) – The Moot Hill of Scone is located within the grounds of Scone Palace, a great house built on the site of the medieval abbey. Few traces of the abbey are visible today, a post-medieval chapel stands on top of the Moot Hill and much of the original prospect is obscured by the palace. Nevertheless, it is an atmospheric site: from the summit of the mound one surveys the heartland of Alba.

NJ 046595 Sueno's Stone, Forres, Moray – The tallest piece of sculpture from this era is now protected in a glass building on the outskirts of Forres. The images of war carved on one side are the most extensive and complex to survive anywhere in Britain. Their meaning remains a matter of keen debate.

NX444403 Whithorn, Dumfries and Galloway – Near the site of the medieval abbey is a museum with a Wne collection of sculpture and a visitor centre which tells the story of one of the most extensive and significant excavations in recent years.

Battle of Inchinnan, Renfrewshire
Columba was not the only saint to have battle magic. The defeat of Somerled was attributed by some to the intervention of St Kentigern.
CHRIS BROWN

Further Reading

Nicholas Aitchison *Macbeth: Man and Myth* (Alan Sutton 1999).

David Breeze, Thomas Clancy, and Richard Welander (eds) *The Stone of Destiny* (Historic Scotland/Society of Antiquaries of Scotland 2002).

Thomas O Clancy (ed) *Triumph Tree: Scotland's Earliest Poetry AD 550–1350* (Canongate Classics 1998).

Barbara Crawford *Scandinavian Scotland* (Leicester University Press 1987).

K S Forsyth (ed) *The Book of Deer 'this Splendid Little Book'* (Four Courts, in press)

Sally M Foster *Picts, Gaels and Scots* (Historic Scotland/Batsford 1996).

Sally M Foster (ed) *The St Andrews Sacrophagus: a Pictish Masterpiece and its International Connections* (Four Courts 1998).

Alan Macquarrie *The Saints of Scotland: Essays in Scottish Church History 450–1093* (John Donald 1997).

Acknowledgements

In general terms I am indebted to my teaching colleagues, Dauvit Broun, Thomas Clancy and Ewan Campbell, because much of what is presented here was first developed in various undergraduate and postgraduate courses which we have taught together. Over the years I have also benefited greatly from discussions with Alex Woolf and Simon Taylor, but probably my most consistent source of sound advice and strong criticism has come from Katherine Forsyth. I owe specific thanks to Gordon Barclay who provided valuable comments at an early stage in the preparation of this text.

HISTORIC SCOTLAND

HISTORIC SCOTLAND safeguards Scotland's built heritage, including its archaeology, and promotes its understanding and enjoyment on behalf of the Secretary of State for Scotland. It undertakes a programme of 'rescue archaeology', from which many of the results are published in this book series.

Scotland has a wealth of ancient monuments and historic buildings, ranging from prehistoric tombs and settlements to remains from the Second World War, and HISTORIC SCOTLAND gives legal protection to the most important, guarding them against damaging changes or destruction. HISTORIC SCOTLAND gives grants and advice to the owners and occupiers of these sites and buildings.

HISTORIC SCOTLAND has a membership scheme which allows access to properties in its care, as well as other benefits.
For information, contact:
0131 668 8999.